Montreal

Chief Editor	Cynthia Clayton Ochterbeck
Senior Editor	M. Linda Lee
Editor	Gaven Watkins
Writer	Paul Glassman
Production Coordinator	Natasha George
Cartography	Peter Wrenn
Photo Editor	Brigitta L. House and Lydia Strong
Proofreader	Gwen Cannon
Layout	Allison M. Simpson
Cover Design	Paris Venise Design
	Paris, 17e

Michelin North America
2540, Boul. Daniel-Johnson, Suite 510
Laval, Québec, H7T 2T9
CANADA
800-423-0485
www.michelintravel.com
email: TheGreenGuide-us@us.michelin.com

Special Sales:

For information regarding bulk sales, customized editions and premium sales, please
contact our Customer Service Departments:

USA – 800-423-0485   **Canada** – 800-361-8236

Michelin Apa Publications Ltd
A joint venture between Michelin and Langenscheidt

ISBN 2-067-12915-5

Printed and bound in Germany

Note to the reader:

While every effort is made to ensure that all information in this guide is correct and
up-to-date, Michelin Apa Publications accepts no liability for any direct, indirect or
consequential losses howsoever caused so far as such can be excluded by law.

Admission prices listed for sights in this guide are for a single adult, unless otherwise
specified.

Welcome to Montreal

Table of Contents

Table of Contents

THE MICHELIN STARS

For more than 75 years, travellers have used the Michelin stars to take the guesswork out of planning a trip. Our star-rating system helps you make the best decision on where to go, what to do, and what to see. A three-star rating means it's one of the "absolutelys"; two stars means it's one of the "should sees"; and one star says it's one of the "must sees" — a must if you have the time.

★★★   Absolutely Must See

★★   Really Must See

★   Must See

Three-Star Sights★★★

Dufferin Terrace★★★ (QC)
Lower Town★★★ (QC)
Old Montreal★★★
Notre Dame Basilica★★★
Quebec City★★★ (QC)
Upper Town★★★ (QC)

Two-Star Sights★★

Château Frontenac★★ (QC)
The Citadel★★ (QC)
Contemporary Art Museum★★
Cosmodôme★★
Eastern Townships★★
Fort Chambly NHS★★
Fortifications of Quebec★★ (QC)
Governors' Walk★★ (QC)
Lachine Canal★★
Laurentians★★
Mary Queen of the World Basilica-Cathedral★★
McCord Museum★★
Montreal Botanical Garden★★
Montreal Museum of Archaeology and History★★
Montreal Museum of Fine Arts★★
Mount Royal Park★★
Museum of Civilization★★ (QC)
Parliament Building★★ (QC)
Place d'Armes★★ (QC)
Place des Arts★★
Place Jacques-Cartier★★
Place Montréal Trust★★
Place Royale★★ (QC)
Place Ville-Marie★★
Quebec Museum of Fine Arts★ (QC)
Quebec Seminary★★ (QC)
Rue Saint-Paul★★
St. Joseph's Oratory★★
Sun Life Building★★
Ursuline Monastery★★ (QC)
West Island and Beyond★★

One-Star Sights★

Anglican Cathedral of the Holy Trinity★ (QC)
Artillery Park NHS★ (QC)
Bank of Montreal★
Biodôme★
Biosphère★
Bonsecours Market★
Brome County Historical Museum★
Canadian Centre for Architecture★
Canadian Railway Museum★
Carré St-Louis★
Chapel of Our Lady of Good Help★ (QC)
Château Dufresne★
Château Ramezay★
Chinatown★
Christ Church Cathedral★
Church of Our Lady of Victories★
Church of St. Jeanne of Chantal★
City Hall★
Complexe Desjardins★
Devil's Falls★
Dominion Square Building★
Dorchester Square★
Fort Lennox NHS★
Fur Trade at Lachine NHS★
Granby Zoo★
Grande Allée★ (QC)
Habitat '67★
Insectarium★
Joliette★
La Ronde★
Lake Brome★
Magog★
Maison Alcan★
Maison du Calvet★
Maisonneuve Monument★
Marc-Aurèle Fortin Museum★
McGill University★
Montreal History Centre★
Montreal Science Centre (iSci)★
Mont-Tremblant Park★
Muskrat Falls★

National Battlefields Park★ (QC)
New City★ (QC)
Notre Dame Island★
Old Courthouse★ (QC)
Old Port★
Old Sulpician Seminary★
Parc du Mont-Orford★
Place d'Armes★ (Montreal)
Plateau Mont-Royal★
Pointe-Claire★
Pointe-du-Moulin Historic Park★
Price Building★
Redpath Museum of Natural History★
Ritz-Carlton Hotel★
Royal Bank of Canada★
Royal Bank Tower★
Rue Crescent★
Rue Saint-Denis★
Rue Saint-Jacques★
Rue Saint-Pierre★ (QC)
Rue Saint-Paul★ (QC)
Sainte-Benoît-du-Lac Abbey★
Sainte-Sauveur-des-Monts★
Sainte-Adèle★
Sainte-Anne-de-Bellevue★
Sainte-Marguerite-du-Lac-Masson★
St. Helen's Island★
Seven Falls of Saint Zénon★
Sir George-Étienne Cartier NHS★
South Shore★
Stewart Hall★
Stewart Museum★
Stock Exchange Tower★
Sutton★
Tour KPMG★
Trestler House★
Victoria Bridge★
Westmount Square★
The Windsor★

The following abbreviations appear in this list:
NHS National Historic Site; QC Quebec City.

Listed below is a selection of Montreal's most popular annual events. Please note that dates may vary from year to year. For more detailed information, contact Tourisme Québec *(514-873-2015 or 877-266-5687; www.bonjourquebec.com)* or Tourisme Montréal *(www.tourisme-montreal.org)*.

January

Fête des Neiges (Winter Carnival) 514-872-6120
Île Ste-Hélène www.fetedesneiges.com

February

Festival Montréal en Lumière
  (Montreal High Lights Festival)
Various locations 514-288-9955 or 888-477-9955
  www.montrealhighlights.com
Rendez-vous du cinéma québécois 514-526-9635
  (Festival of Quebec films)
Various locations www.rvcq.com

March

International Children's Film Festival 514-842-7750
Cinéma Beaubien www.fifem.com
St. Patrick's Day Parade
Rue Ste-Catherine

April

Blue Metropolis – International Literary Festival
Hotel Delta Centre-Ville 514-937-2538
  www.blue-met-bleu.com
Vues d'Afrique (African and Creole Film Festival)
Cinéma Beaubien 514-284-3322
  www.vuesdafrique.org

May

Festival TransAmériques 514-842-0704
  (Theatre and Dance Festival of the Americas)
Various locations www.fta.qc.ca
Montreal Bike Fest 450-521-8687
Montreal streets and parks www.velo.qc.ca

June

First Peoples' Festival 514-278-4040
Various locations www.nativelynx.qc.ca
Fringe Festival 514-849-3378
Various theatres www.montrealfringe.ca
Grand Prix du Canada 514-350-0000
Île Notre-Dame www.grandprix.ca
Mondial de la bière (Beer Festival) 514-722-9640
Windsor Station www.festivalmondialbiere.qc.ca

World Fireworks Competition   514-397-2000
Île Ste-Hélène (through Aug)
www.internationaldesfeuxloto-quebec.com

July

Canada Day   514-866-9164
Old Port   www.celafete.ca

Festival Juste pour rire (Just for Laughs Festival)
Latin Quarter   514-845-2322 or 888-244-3155
www.hahaha.com

Festival International de Jazz de Montréal
Place des Arts area   514-871-1881 or 888-515-0515
www.montrealjazzfest.com

Nuits d'Afrique (African Nights)   514-499-3462
Various locations   www.festivalnuitsdafrique.com

August

Divers/Cité (Gay Pride)   514-285-4011
Rues Berri & Ste-Catherine   www.diverscite.org

La Fête des Enfants (Children's Festival)   514-872-0060
Maisonneuve Park
www.ville.montreal.qc.ca/fetedesenfants

Les FrancoFolies (French-language comedy and music)
Place des Arts area   514-876-8989 or 888-444-9114
www.francofolies.com

Montreal World Film Festival   514-848-3883
Downtown cinemas   www.ffm-montreal.org

September

Marathon international de Montréal   514-879-1027
www.marathondemontreal.com

Fall Festival-Orgue et couleurs (Organ and Colours)
Various locations   www.orgueetcouleurs.com

October

Black and Blue Festival (Gay Celebration)
Olympic Stadium   514-875-7026
www.bbcm.org

November

Coup de Coeur Francophone (French-language music)
Various locations   www.coupdecoeur.qc.ca

Cinemania Film Festival   514-878-0082
Cinéma Impérial   www.cinemaniafilmfestival.com

December

Victorian Christmas   514-283-2282
Sir George-Étienne Cartier
National Historic Site   www.pc.gc.ca/cartier

Must Know: Practical Information

WHEN TO GO

Summer is the most popular season to visit Montreal. There are long hours of daylight, an intense schedule of free festivals, and only occasional spells of hot, humid weather. Late spring and early fall are also pleasant, with many outdoor activities still available. And the pleasures of a sunny Indian summer afternoon in October are not to be missed. Then there is the special experience of a winter city, as Montreal moves indoors and underground for many of its daily activities, and outdoors for its recreation, to skating rinks and cross-country ski trails and wintry celebrations. Sub-arctic chills are inevitable, but also brief, and there are thaws and even rain. In winter, facilities are uncrowded and room rates fall.

Seasonal Temperatures in Montreal *(recorded at Trudeau International Airport)*

	Jan	Apr	July	Oct
Avg. High	-6°C / 21°F	11°C / 52°F	26°C / 79°F	13°C / 55°F
Avg. Low	-14°C / 7°F	1°C / 34°F	16°C / 61°F	5°C / 41°F

PLANNING YOUR TRIP

Before you go, contact Tourisme-Québec, which handles inquiries from outside the city, and will send information tailored to your request; or go to the Tourism Montreal Web site.

Tourisme Québec
P. O. Box 979, Montreal, QC Canada H3C 2W3
1010 Rue Ste-Catherine Ouest, Bureau 400,
Montreal, QC Canada H3B 1G2
514-873-2015 or 877-266-5687
www.bonjourquebec.com

Tourisme Montréal
1555 Rue Peel Ste. 600,
Montreal, QC Canada H3A 3L8
www.tourisme-montreal.org

Visitor Centres

Infotouriste Centre
1001 Rue du Square-Dorchester
Open year-round daily 9am–6pm;
(Jun–Labour Day 8:30am–7:30pm)
Métro Peel, green line

Montreal Online

In addition to the tourism bureau sites shown, here are some Web sites to help you plan your trip:
www.ville.montreal.qc.ca
www.quaysoftheoldport.com/
www.vieux.montreal.qc.ca
www.canada.com/cityguides/montreal
www.quartierlatin.ca

In the News

You'll find the most complete listings of films, theatre and exhibitions in English in the Saturday Weekend sections of *The Gazette*, available at all newsstands, and online at *www.montrealgazette.com*. Free entertainment weeklies, with extensive listings of music, theater, gay, and youth-oriented events, include *The Mirror (www.montreal-mirror.com)* and *Hour (www.hour.ca)*. These are often available at hotels and many Métro stations. Coverage is generally more detailed in the French-language media, including *La Presse (www.cyberpresse.ca)* and the more highbrow *Le Devoir (www.ledevoir.com)*. The main free French-language weekly is *Voir (www.voir.ca)*.

Infotouriste Centre
174 Rue Notre-Dame Est, Old Montreal
Open year-round daily 9am–5pm;
(Jun–Labour Day to 7pm; closed Mon–Tue Nov–Mar)
Metro Place-d'Armes, orange line

Useful Passes

Unlimited **transit passes** are a great value for intensive on-and-off bus and subway travel *(see Getting Around)*. The **Montreal Museums Pass** *(see Museums)* provides unlimited entry for three days, and an optional bargain transit pass.

GETTING THERE

By Plane – **Trudeau (Dorval) International Airport (YUL)** is 14km/9mi from downtown *(514-394-7377 or 800-465-1213; www.admtl.com)*. Taxis have a fixed $35 fare to downtown. Coaches operate to the **Central Bus Station** station *(777 Rue de la Gauchetière Ouest; 514-842-2281)* with shuttle connections to major hotels.

By Train – Daily service to Montreal's **Central Station** *(Gare Centrale, Rue de la Gauchetière between Université & Mansfield)* is provided by **VIA Rail** from major cities in Canada *(888-842-7245; www.viarail.ca)* and by **Amtrak** from New York City and Albany *(800-872-7245; www.amtrak.com)*. **Commuter trains** serve suburbs on and off Montreal island from Central Station and from **Windsor Station** *(Rue de la Gauchetière at Peel)*.

By Bus – Montreal's **Central Bus Station** *(Gare Centrale d'autobus, 505 de Maisonneuve Est; 514-842-2281)* is the departure point for all buses. For travel from the US, contact **Greyhound** *(800-229-9424; www.greyhound.com)* or **Adirondack Trailways** *(www.trailwaysny.com; 800-858-8555)*. For travel within the province of Quebec, contact **Orléans Express** *(514-842-2281; www.orleansexpress.com)*. For travel from elsewhere in Canada, contact **Canadian Greyhound** *(www.greyhound.ca; 800-661-8747)*.

By Car – Major expressways connect Montreal with New York City (Autoroute 15 and I-87), Boston (I-89 and I-93), and with Toronto and Quebec City. Bridges connect the island city with the mainland.

Car Rental Company	Reservations	Internet
Alamo	800-327-9633	www.alamo.com
Avis	800-331-1212	www.avis.com
Budget	800-268-8900	www.budget.com
Dollar	800-800-4000	www.dollar.com
Enterprise	800-736-8222	www.enterprise.com
Hertz	800-263-0600	www.hertz.com
National	800-227-7368	www.nationalcar.com
Thrifty	800-847-4389	www.thrifty.com

Must Know: Practical Information

GETTING AROUND

The Street System – Most streets bear names, not numbers, and signs use French terminology (*"rue"* for "street," usually dropped when giving an address, and *"est"* or *"ouest"* for east or west of Boulevard St-Laurent). On streets running roughly northward, buildings are numbered starting from the St. Lawrence River. Some street names have widely used informal English equivalents *(Rue de la Montagne/Mountain Street)*.

By Car – No car is needed to get around the compact central area, and in fact, it's best to avoid dealing with congestion, meters and pay stations, confusing signs and parking regulations. **Right turns on red lights are not permitted in Montreal.** Use of seat belts is required. Safety seats are required for children under 18kg/40lbs; a booster seat is required for heavier children up to age eight. Drivers must yield to buses entering their lane from the right. Lanes are reserved for taxis and buses on major streets during **rush hours** *(7am–9am & 4:30pm–6:30pm)*. Some parking spaces are reserved for the handicapped, deliveries and diplomats. Cars parked illegally may be ticketed, towed or immobilized.

On Foot – Montreal is a compact city, with a central area only about 2km/1.24mi square and few challenging slopes. Walking is pleasant during most of the year. In winter, icy sidewalks can be a hazard, and appropriate clothing is a must. Underground passageways *(see p 32)* offer sheltered routes when it's cold or rainy or humid outside. A map is handy to help you find your way and to locate passageways and named streets. The free public transit map shows approximate street numbers.

Public Transportation

The **Societé des Transports de Montréal** *(514-786-4636; www.stm.info)* operates the island-wide subway and bus network. Free transfers are permitted between the two modes. Cash fare is $2.50, a strip of six tickets costs $12 (half-fare for children under 12; children under age 5 ride free). Unlimited passes are available to visitors April to October at most downtown Métro stations (and at the Berri, Peel and Bonaventure stations all year) for $9 *(one day)* and $17 *(three days; $45 with museum pass)*. The $19 weekly pass *(Sun–Sat)* available at any Métro station is the best value. Schedules are posted at many bus stops, and can be checked on the Internet.

City Buses – Buses operate throughout downtown and the outer areas of the city. Use a pass or ticket, or pay a higher cash price. Most routes begin operation by 6am and end shortly after midnight. There are some rush-hour-only services, and hourly service on a limited number of all-night routes.

Taxis – Many taxis cruise Montreal streets or operate from taxi stands, charging $3.15 to start and $1.45 per kilometre. Flat rates can be negotiated for long trips. There is no uniform taxi colour, but available cabs have an illuminated roof light. Major cab companies in Montreal include: **Atlas Taxi** *(514-485-8585)*; **Diamond Taxi** *(514-273-6331)*; and **Montreal Taxi Coop** *(514-725-9885)*.

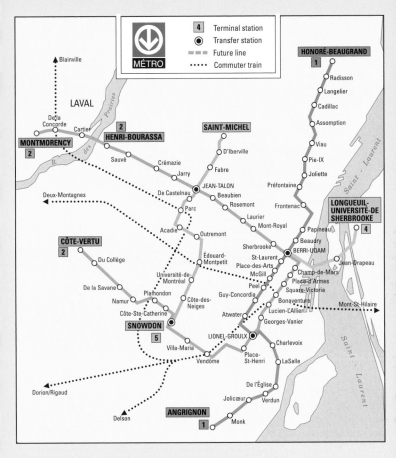

Subway – *See map above.* Montreal's subterranean commuter train system is the **Métro**, and its arrow-in-a-circle logo, white on blue, prominently identifies stations. Two lines, the orange and the green, cross downtown from east to west, intersecting at either end of the central area. Métro trains operate from about 5:30am to 12:30am most days. Fares *(p 12)* are based on a flat rate. Buy subway tickets at station ticket booths or at 7-11 convenience stores (called *dépanneurs*).

Area Codes

All of Montreal island uses the 514 area code; the surrounding off-island suburbs use the 450 area code. Include the area code (without the long-distance "1" prefix) when dialing all calls. Before you leave home, check with your carrier to make sure your cell phone will operate in Canada.

Montreal: 514
Off-island suburbs: 450
Quebec City: 418

Important Numbers

Important Numbers	
Emergency (police/fire/ambulance, 24hrs)	**911**
Police (non-emergency)	514-280-2222
Hotel Medical Services for visitors	800-468-3537
Community Health Centre and Medical Referral (CLSC)	514-934-0354
24-hour Pharmacy:	
Pharmaprix, 5122 Côte-des-Neiges	514-738-8464
Weather	514-283-3010

TIPS FOR SPECIAL VISITORS

Disabled Travellers – All museums and public buildings in Montreal have ramps and automatic doors for visitors in wheelchairs. Most major hotels provide accessible and adapted rooms. Disabled access is not required by law, however, so there are some exceptions.

Passengers travelling from the US who need assistance with train or bus travel should give advance notice to **Amtrak** *(800-872-7245 or 800-523-6590/TDD; www.amtrak.com)* or **Greyhound** *(800-752-4841/US, 800-661-8747/Canada, or 800-345-3109/TDD; www.greyhound.com)*. Request assistance when reserving on **VIA Rail** in Canada *(888-842-7245 or though any ticket office)*. Wheelchairs may be reserved by calling the Orléans Express bus company *(800-419-8735)*. Make reservations for hand-controlled cars in advance with the rental company.

Accessible **public transportation** on low-floor buses is provided on the main routes, only at stops displaying the universal accessibility symbol. Visitors may also access the separate handicapped-only bus network; to arrange airport pickup, call 514-280-8211 before visiting. The subway *(Métro)* is **not** accessible to wheelchairs. Visitors can request an adapted van when phoning for a taxi.

Local Lowdown – The following organizations provide detailed information about access for the disabled in the province of Quebec:

- Kéroul, an organization that promotes travel for the disabled, publishes *Québec accessible ($20; 514-252-3104; www.keroul.qc.ca)*.
- The Canadian government provides information about accessible travel on its Web site: *www.accesstotravel.gc.ca/main-e.asp*.

Senior Citizens – Many hotels, attractions and restaurants offer discounts to visitors age 62 or older (proof of age may be required). The **AARP** (formerly the American Association of Retired Persons, *601 E St. NW, Washington, DC 20049; 202-424-3410; www.aarp.com)* arranges discounts for its members, as does Canada's **Association for the Fifty-Plus** (CARP, *Suite 1304, 27 Queen St. E., Toronto, ON M5C 2M6; 416-363-8748; www.50plus.com)*.

LANGUAGES

French is the official language of Quebec province and the majority language in Montreal. Businesses are generally required to use French in their operations and on signs. All road signs are in French. English is widely understood, especially downtown. You can usually find assistance in English, either in person or when calling.

Glossary

In the **Must Sees Montreal** text, we include names in English and French, where applicable. Knowing a few words in Canadian French will come in handy:

yes - oui; **no** - non

please - s'il vous plaît

welcome - bienvenue

lunch - dîner

hello, good morning - bonjour

goodbye - bye

how much? - combien?

where? - où?

I don't understand - Je ne comprends pas

exit - sortie

thank you - merci

breakfast - déjeuner

dinner - souper

expressway - autoroute

gasoline - essence

collect call - appel à frais virés

subway - Métro

Do you speak English? - Parlez-vous anglais?

FOREIGN VISITORS

In addition to local tourism offices, visitors may obtain information from the nearest Canadian embassy or consulate in their country of residence. For further information on Canadian embassies, consult the Web site of the Canadian Department of Foreign Affairs and International Trade: *www.dfait-maeci.gc.ca.*

Entry requirements — As of January 2007, citizens of the US need a valid passport or Air NEXUS card to visit Canada and return by air. A driver's license and a birth certificate together are currently accepted to enter Canada and return to the US by land or sea. Parents bringing children into Canada are strongly advised to carry birth certificates. As of 2008, only a passport or secure passport card will be accepted to return to the US. All other visitors to Canada must have a valid passport and, in some cases, a visa *(see list of countries at www.cic.gc.ca/english/visit/visas.html)*. No vaccinations are necessary. For entry into Canada via the US, all persons other than US citizens or legal residents are required to present a valid passport. Check with the Canadian embassy or consulate in your home country about entry regulations and proper travel documents.

Canada Customs — Visitors over 18 entering Quebec may bring 1.14 litres of liquor or 1.5 litres of wine or 24 cans of beer without paying duty or taxes. Tobacco is limited to 200 cigarettes or 196 grams/7 ounces of loose product. Gifts totaling $60 Canadian may be brought in duty-free. All prescription drugs should be clearly labeled and for personal use only; carry a copy of the prescription. Canada has stringent legislation on firearms—do not bring any weapons to the border *(for information, contact the Canadian Firearms Centre, Ottawa, Ontario K1A 1M6 Canada; 800-731-4000; www.cfc-ccaf.gc.ca).*

Money and Currency Exchange — United States currency is widely accepted, but it's best *not* to use it, given poor exchange rates. Currency exchanges are available at the airports, downtown *(Rue Peel at Ste-Catherine)*, and at many banks. It's easiest to use credit cards for purchases or to withdraw money at a bank machine. Report lost or stolen credit cards to: American Express *(800-528-4800)*; Diners Club *(800-234-6377)*; Master Card *(800-307-7309)*; or Visa *(800-336-8472)*. Discover cards are not widely accepted in Canada.

The $ symbol in this book indicates Canadian currency. All prices shown are in Canadian dollars.

Driving in Canada – Drivers from the US may use valid state-issued licenses. Visitors from elsewhere should obtain an International Driving Permit through their national automobile association in order to rent a car. Drivers must carry a vehicle registration card or rental contract and proof of automobile insurance at all times. Gasoline is sold by the litre. Vehicles are driven on the right-hand side of the road.

Electricity – Voltage in Canada is 120 volts AC, 60 Hz, as in the US. Appliances from outside North America require adapters to Canadian voltage and flat-blade outlets.

Taxes – Prices displayed in Canada generally do not include federal and provincial sales taxes (totaling 14 percent in Quebec). Sales tax applies to postage stamps, some food items and many services.

Time Zone – Montreal is located in the Eastern Standard Time (EST) zone, five hours behind Greenwich Mean Time.

Tipping – Service charges are not included in restaurant prices. It's customary to give a small gift of money—a tip—for services rendered to waiters or taxi drivers (up to 15% of fare), porters ($1 per bag) and chambermaids ($1 per day).

Weights and Measures – Canada is officially on the metric system. Gasoline is sold by the litre and produce by the kilo, while road distances are displayed in kilometres (multiply by 0.6 for approximate equivalent in miles) and temperatures in degrees Celsius.

Measurement Equivalents

Degrees Fahrenheit	95°	86°	77°	68°	59°	50°	41°	32°	23°	14°
Degrees Celsius	35°	30°	25°	20°	15°	10°	5°	0°	-5°	-10°

1 ounce	= 28 grams (gm)		**1 mile**	= 1.6 kilometres (km)
1 inch	= 2.54 centimetres (cm)		**1 quart**	= 0.94 litres
1 foot	= 30.48 centimetres		**1 gallon**	= 3.78 litres

ACCOMMODATIONS

For a list of suggested accommodations, see Must Stay.

Reservations Services:

Hospitality Canada – 888-338-9839; www.hospitality-canada.com/english.html.
Downtown B&B Network – 800-267-5180; www.bbmontreal.qc.ca.
Montreal Reservation B&B Network – 800-917-0747; www.montrealreservation.com.
Relais Montréal Hospitalité – 800-363-9635; www.martha-pearson.

Hostels – The Montreal International Youth Hostel *(1030 Mackay; 514-843-3317; www.hostellingmontreal.com)* offers dormitory beds for under $26 all year to holders of Hostelling International card.

Major hotel and motel chains with locations in or near Montreal include:

Property	Phone	Web site
Best Western	800-780-7234	www.bestwestern.com
Comfort, Clarion & Quality Inns	800-424-6423	www.choicehotels.com
Days Inn	800-329-7466	www.daysinn.com
Delta Hotels	877-814-7706	www.deltahotels.com
Fairmont	800-441-1414	www.fairmont.com
Hilton	800-445-8667	www.hilton.com
Holiday Inn	800-465-4329	www.holiday-inn.com
Hyatt	800-233-1234	www.hyatt.com
InterContinental	800-327-0200	www.ichotelsgroup.com
Sheraton	800-325-3535	www.sheraton.com
Marriott	800-228-9290	www.marriott.com
Méridien	800-543-4300	www.lemeridien.com
Omni	800-843-6664	www.omnihotels.com
Ramada Inns	800-272-6232	www.ramada.com
Ritz-Carlton	800-241-3333	www.ritzcarlton.com

Many hotels in all categories are listed on: www.tourisme-montreal.org.

SPORTS

Montreal is a great place to be a spectator at sporting events. The city's major professional sports teams include:

Sport/Team	Season	Venue	info#/tickets#	Web site
Hockey Montreal Canadiens (National Hockey League)	Oct–Apr	Bell Centre	514-790-1245 800-361-4595 800-678-5440	www.canadiens.com
Canadian Football Montreal Alouettes (Canadian Football League)	June–Oct	Molson Stadium	514-871-2255/ 514-790-1245	www.montreal alouettes.com
Soccer Montreal Impact	Apr-Sept	Claude-Robillard Stadium	514-328-3668	www.montrealimpact. com

Montreal

Joie de Vivre in North America: Montreal

American-style efficiency, Canadian courtesy, Old World charm, the beauty of the French language in everyday life, Latin attitudes and fabulous food: Circumstances, peoples and geography have combined to make Montreal a metropolis like no other. It is a summer city with great gardens and parks, and a winter city that moves indoors and underground to overcome the climate, and outdoors to challenge it. It is a major port for the eastern half of the continent, and a high-tech capital. It is a city hurtling into the future while confident in its traditions, where fashion and manners count as much as personal achievement.

Montreal, peaceful and mannered today, grew out of conquests, colonization and conflicts. This island in the St. Lawrence attracted the attention of French explorers, notably Jacques Cartier, who visited in 1535. Samuel de Champlain established a fur-trading outpost here in 1611, and a mission, Ville-Marie de Montréal, followed in 1642.

Despite failed crops, harsh winters, disease, and attacks by the native inhabitants, gradually, a French way of life was transplanted to the New World. Religious orders were in the vanguard, tending to farming as well as souls.

Remote as it was, New France became involved in conflicts with England. Full-scale war erupted in 1756. The clifftop fortress at Quebec City gave way in 1759, and Montreal succumbed a year later.

England now ruled North America, but it was only a change of management at the top. Under the Quebec Act of 1774, the Catholic religion was tolerated in Canada, and French civil law continued in effect. When the American Revolutionary army captured Montreal in 1775, the soldiers found a population largely unwilling to join its cause.

Under the British, Montreal began to develop on the parallel tracks that have characterized the city to this day. French Canadians largely continued to cultivate the land or enter the priesthood or the law. Business and investment became the realm of English and Scottish immigrants, and later, of Tories fleeing the newly independent United States.

The old city walls were demolished. Lumber and mineral exports picked up the slack when the fur trade declined. In 1825, the Lachine Canal opened, bypassing rapids on the St. Lawrence River. Goods could now be landed in Montreal for shipment to the Great Lakes. Railroads and industry followed. Trains chugged in from the US over the Victoria Bridge in 1847, and by 1886, rails ran from Montreal to Vancouver.

Resentments simmered among the poorer French, who held no real political power. Rebellion broke out in 1837, and was quickly put down. Montreal became the capital of United Canada, but only until 1849, when rioters torched the parliament building on Place D'Youville.

Montreal shrugged, and continued to grow, expanding its boundaries to take in neighbouring villages. By the 20C, it had become again a largely French-speaking city, and a new revolution was in the works. French-speakers were no longer content to stay on a separate track. They took political control of the city, and entered all fields of commerce. Some leaders even called for secession from Canada.

Through the 20C, Montreal became a leader in urban planning in cold climates. It rose upward, and plunged underground, into indoor commercial complexes and a state-of-the-art subway system. It dazzled the world as the host of a world's fair, Expo '67, and the Olympic Games in 1976.

But it also started on a gradual decline. After the St. Lawrence Seaway opened in 1959, ocean shipping began to bypass the city. Industry and commerce shifted westward. Secessionists took control of the provincial government, and English-speaking residents began to leave. Toronto, once a junior rival, began to outgrow, out-ship, and outpace Montreal.

Montreal has taken stock, faced up to the challenges, mended its many strains, and continued to be . . . Montreal! The streets are safe and filled with strollers at all hours, even into the winter. Relatively low rents and start-up costs attract offbeat businesses and artists from all over. International organizations and corporations take advantage of workers who speak more than one language, a moderate cost of living, a relaxed pace, excellent food, and a perfect mix of the familiar and the exotic. And so do many visitors.

Fast Facts

- Following annexations in 2002, Montreal covers most of an island measuring 50km by 30km (31mi by 18.6mi) where the Ottawa River joins the St. Lawrence.

- Two-thirds of Montrealers speak French as their first language.

- About 20 percent of the population of 1,600,000 (1,800,000 on the island) is foreign-born; many more are first-generation Québecois.

- The cross atop Mount Royal *(Mont-Royal)* is Montreal's signature, a monument to the missionaries and religious orders that shaped Quebec for much of its history.

L andmark or historic site? Given Montreal's rich past, the lines sometimes blur. But there are plenty of *tours de force* in Montreal's urban fabric, both old and new.

Notre Dame Basilica★★★ *Basilique Notre-Dame*

110 Rue Notre-Dame Ouest. 514-842-2925. www.basiliquenddm.org. $4. Open Mon–Fri 8am–4:30pm, Sat 8am–4:15pm, Sun 12:30–4:15pm. Métro Place d'Armes, orange line.

Notre Dame is where celebrities mark their milestones, whether they attend Mass regularly or not. Pop diva Céline Dion was married inside. Pierre Elliott Trudeau's funeral ended with a rendition of *O Canada* on the carillon as an honour guard of Mounties bore his casket down the steps (while Jimmy Carter chatted with Fidel Castro). On both joyful and solemn occasions, Montrealers put aside their differences and come together at the Basilica of Notre Dame.

Having lost their secular power under the British, the Sulpicians sought to reinforce their religious prominence with a grand cathedral where all the faithful in Montreal could gather. They commissioned an Irish American, James O'Donnell, who designed twin-towered Notre Dame in Gothic Revival style. Construction began in 1824, and the Basilica opened in 1829, but it wasn't yet finished—work continued until 1870. The cathedral marked the first large-scale use of limestone in Montreal, which became a signature building material in the city.

The Cathedral – Outside, the church is an expression of grandeur and a projection of power; inside, it is opulent and spiritual at the same time, and simply overpowering in the otherworldly play of natural light flowing in through its three rose windows. The woodwork is sumptuous, painted and gilt, cascading into niches filled with saints. Decorations are largely of carved pine and oak. The lower stained-glass windows, crafted in Limoges, France, tell the story of Montreal. The **organ** is one of the largest anywhere. At the rear of the cathedral, the modern **Sacred Heart Chapel** contrasts sharply with the rest of Notre Dame. The chapel was reconstructed in contemporary style, with light wood paneling, following a fire in 1978.

Sound and Light

Et la lumière fut (And There Was Light) celebrates Montreal's history and heritage with lights, sound effects, and screens, curtains and scenery that magically disappear after each performance. Altogether, it's a high-tech event in a traditional setting. *Tue–Thu 6:30pm, Fri 6:30 & 8:30pm, Sat 7 & 8:30pm, also Tue–Thu 8:30pm in summer; tickets are $10 at the Basilica shop, 514-842-2925, ext. 226, or www.admission.com.*

Place des Arts★★

175 Rue Ste-Catherine Ouest. 514-842-2112. www.pdarts.com. Open year-round daily and for performances. Métro Place des Arts, green line.

In the 1960s, the city of Montreal selected what used to be a no-man's land for its performance centre, between the English business section in the west and the traditional French cultural institutions along Rue Saint-Denis. The first of the government-sponsored mega-projects of Montreal, it was followed by Complexe Guy-Favreau nearby and the monumental concrete **Olympic Stadium**, built for the 1976 Olympic Games.

Events flow around the fountains and through the multilevel plazas of Place des Arts during the milder months and even in the middle of winter. Glass walls allow a view inside to Salle Wilfrid Pelletier and the **Contemporary Art Museum★★** *(Musée d'Art Contemporain de Montréal; see Museums).*

Salle Wilfrid Pelletier – At the north end of the plaza, the large columned building with a curving façade is home to the Orchestre Symphonique (Montreal Symphony Orchestra), as well as the Opéra de Montréal and Les Grands Ballets. Its stark interior is relieved by tapestries and sculptures by Anne Kahane and Louis Archambault.

Théâtre Maisonneuve – Located near Rue Sainte-Catherine, this large performance facility lies directly above the **Théâtre Jean-Duceppe**. The floating floor of one is also the moveable ceiling of the space below—but the construction is such that nobody is aware of the activity in the other hall. To reach any of these, or the smaller **Studio Théâtre** or **Cinquième Salle**, enter the indoor passageway that descends from Rue Sainte-Catherine *(see Performing Arts).*

What's Doing at the *Place*?

Any time the weather's mild, there's sure to be a festival at Place des Arts. Stages are set up in the surrounding streets during the Jazz Festival, and the open areas are filled with souvenir shops, refreshment stands, stages, inflatables, and people, people, people. During the annual Film Festival, spectators unfold chairs and set down blankets to get comfy and watch an outdoor movie. And it didn't take too much effort to convince several hundred Montrealers to shed their clothes a few years ago and pose for a piece of performance art that is currently making the rounds of the world's art museums as photographic blowups.

Mary Queen of the World Basilica-Cathedral★★
Basilique-Cathédrale Marie-Reine-du-Monde

1085 Rue de la Cathédrale at Boul. René-Lévesque. 514-866-1661.
www.cathedralecatholiquedemontreal.org. Open year-round 7:30am–6pm.
Tours in summer only. Métro Bonaventure, orange line.

Rarely does a city have more than one Catholic cathedral. But the establishment of a large Catholic church in the very centre of 19C Montreal's English-dominated business district was a political and cultural statement by the bishop of the day, Ignace Bourget.

And what a statement! Plans were unblushingly copied from those of St. Peter's in Rome, reduced to half scale. Work began in 1870, but with money coming in and running out, it was not until 1894 that the cathedral formally opened.

The Building – Even on a reduced scale, "St.-Peter's-in-Montreal" is massive, successfully competing for attention with some of Montreal's tallest buildings nearby. Copper-plated statues in the pediment represent the patron saints of local parishes. Inside, the gold-plated copper canopy is a replica of one in St. Peter's in Rome. Check out the woodwork and the series of paintings that reveal French-Canadian history.

Place Montréal Trust★★

1500 Ave. McGill College at Rue Ste-Catherine. 514-843-8000. Open year-round
Mon–Tue 10am–6pm (Jun–Aug until 8pm), Wed–Fri 10am–9pm, Sat 10am–5pm,
Sun 10am–5pm. Métro McGill, green line.

Dating from 1989, the Montréal Trust tower is a remarkable intersection of cylindrical volumes, and of materials old and new. Flat surfaces are mostly of rose-colored marble, divided by cylinders of glass and polished aluminum—the one indistinguishable from the other—reflecting the sky and clouds and surrounding cityscape. The effect, on a sunny day, is a remarkable illusion of translucence and depth.

Inside, Place Montréal Trust is dedicated to materialism. It extends well below street level and connects with the Underground City. The purpose is shopping—there are scores of boutiques—but the architectural drama of five storeys of galleries, the play of water from one of the largest indoor fountains anywhere, the street scene visible in any weather through expanses of plate glass, and refreshment at numerous eateries may entice you to stay longer.

Place Ville-Marie★★

Ave. McGill College at Rue Cathcart. 514-861-9393. Métro Bonaventure, orange line.

Place Ville-Marie (PVM in local usage) marked a Canadian advance in urban design when it opened in 1962. Predecessors such as the Dominion Square Building included interior shopping along arcades. But Place Ville-Marie reached out underground to connect with adjacent urban nodes, such as Central Station. On the surface, it blurred boundaries, encouraging pedestrians to flow into its plazas, and onward to its shopping arcades, through multiple wide doorways. Aluminum sheathing marked a departure from stone, brick and steel surfacing materials.

Long delayed by lack of funds, Place Ville-Marie was one of the greatest construction projects in Canada in its day, filling in a gaping basin left in the centre of downtown by railway tunnel construction.

Beacon of Montreal – Place Ville-Marie now soars over Montreal in counterpoint to the great mass of Mount Royal. The cruciform plan of the Royal Bank Tower reflects the cross of faith that crowns the mountain. At night, the cross shines on Mount Royal, as does the beacon atop Place Ville-Marie.

The Buildings and the Plan – The **Royal Bank Tower★** *(Tour Banque-Royale)*, at 42 storeys, is the largest of PVM's buildings, designed by the firm of I. M. Pei. Smaller buildings partially flank the complex. Generous street-level interruptions allow the unimpeded flow of pedestrians.

Visiting – Just walk in! Enter Place Ville-Marie from the freestanding glassed-in entry on the plaza, through doors on Rue Cathcart or Rue University, or by passageway from Central Station or the Eaton Centre. Shops, restaurants and occasional entertainment are sufficient to keep you occupied for hours; light flowing in through the skylights makes the ambience downright cheery.

Eaton Centre

Ave. McGill College at Rue Ste-Catherine. Just across Avenue McGill College and a few steps past the corner (going eastward, north side) is the earlier **Eaton Centre**, another multistorey, contemporary shopping complex. It adjoins the stately Art Deco building of the legendary **Eaton Department Store**, which fell victim to down-market competition and closed its doors a few years ago. The space has been taken over by other retailers, and traces of the original interior styling remain.

St. Joseph's Oratory★★   *Oratoire Saint-Joseph*

3800 Chemin Queen-Mary. 514-733-8211. www.saint-joseph.org. Votive Chapel open year-round daily 6am–9:30pm; Basilica open year-round daily 7am–5:30pm & for late Masses; Way of the Cross Gardens open May–Sept. Métro Côte-des-Neige, blue line.

No other religious site in Montreal comes close to St. Joseph's in massive size or in the devotion of its visitors. Brother André (1845–1937), who began his religious life as a porter in a school, promoted the healing power of praying to St. Joseph. He attracted a following who threw off their crutches and afflictions in ever greater numbers. Brother André was beatified in 1982.

The Oratory – Construction of the Oratory—literally, a place of prayer—began in 1924 on the northern slope of Westmount Mountain. The massive project was interrupted a number of times, finally coming under the direction of re-nowned Benedictine architect Paul Bellot. It was not completed until 1967.

You can reach the Romanesque Oratory on foot by a series of staircases ascending its terraced lawns (or you can drive). It rises to 154m/505ft above the city. The space under the dome soars to 60m/198ft, while the tip of its crowning cross stands 97m/320ft above the ground.

Inside, St. Joseph's is stark and powerful, barely adorned and suitable to private prayer and meditation. The carillon is from France, originally intended for installation in the Eiffel Tower *(performances Thu & Fri noon & 3pm, Sat–Sun noon & 2:30pm)*. Not incidentally, given the Oratory's height and location, commanding views extend from the terrace northward over the city to the Laurentian Mountains.

The Votive Chapel – The most moving testimony to the powers of St. Joseph is the collection of canes and crutches left by those cured through prayer. Enlarged several times to accommodate his followers, Brother André's original **chapel** has been restored to its appearance in 1904.

Way of the Cross – The traditional pilgrims' route along the hillside is marked by 42 statues designed by Louis Parent, one of Quebec's most noted contem-porary sculptors. The statue of St. John at Gethsemane is considered an Art Deco masterpiece.

Sun Life Building★★

1155 Rue Metcalfe. Métro Peel, green line, or Bonaventure, orange line.

Towering over the east side of Dorchester Square, the massive and bankerly Sun Life Building was the largest in the then-British Empire when it was completed in 1918. Designed by the firm of Darling and Pearson, the monumental edifice sports columns and pediments that make reference to classical architecture but they are out of proportion—the effect is something like a cubist painting. It's only a step from the Sun Life Building to architectural designs that recognize the skyscraper as a class unto itself.

Bastion for Britain – Headquarters of a major insurance company, secure in fact as well as symbolically, the Sun Life Building came to hold the gold reserves of several European countries during World War II, as well as the crown jewels of Great Britain. Sun Life angered many people when the company moved its headquarters to Toronto after secessionists carried the 1978 provincial elections. The company has since stuck to business and marketed itself more benignly, as *la Sun Life du Canada.*

Bank of Montreal★ *Banque de Montréal*

119 Rue St-Jacques Ouest. 514-877-6810. Métro Place-d'Armes, orange line.

There have always been money-lenders, but the Bank of Montreal was the first proper bank in Canada. By 1847, it was dominant enough to establish a new head office on Place d'Armes, the most prestigious location of the day. British architect John Wells designed a domed secular temple that imitated the Pantheon in Rome. John Steele later added the sculptures on the pediment. The premises were enlarged in 1901 while preserving the dome as the centrepiece. A vast, columned hall still provides retail services. To the left of the entry, a one-room **museum** displays antique adding machines and photos of banking operations in times past *(open year-round Mon–Fri 10am–4pm).*

Building as Logo – Early on, the bank realized the value of architecture as symbol and brand. Branches began to appear in major centres across Canada, differing in detail, but always faithful to the dome and columns as symbols of strength, security and reliability.

The Biodôme★

4777 Ave. Pierre-de-Coubertin. 514-868-3000. www.biodome.qc.ca. Open year-round Tue–Sun 9am–5pm (summer until 6pm). $11.75. Métro Viau, green line.

Pack up the world's climates and place them under a dome—a former Olympic cycling track—for all the world to see. It sounds like the project of a mad scientist, but it's fairly amazing in reality. At the Biodôme, caimans and piranhas, penguins and parrots, vines and ferns, swim, fly, grow and climb through the tropics, the Laurentian forest, the St. Lawrence River and the refrigerated Arctic.

A **free shuttle** provides transportation between the Biodôme, the Insectarium, Botanical Garden, Olympic Park, and Viau Métro station.

City Hall★   *Hôtel de Ville*

275 Rue Notre-Dame Est. 514-872-0077. Open for self-guided tours Mon–Fri 8am–5pm; group guided tours Mon–Fri 9am–4pm by appointment. Closed holidays. Métro Champ-de-Mars, orange line.

Montreal's City Hall is a solid, stone-clad building with a mansard roof, the first major building in Montreal to adopt the Second Empire style that was all the rage toward the end of the 19C. Completed in 1878, it was raised one storey in 1922 during reconstruction after a fire.

Controversies surrounding City Hall are usually of local concern only. But in 1967, President Charles de Gaulle of France called out *"Vive le Québec Libre"* ("Long live free Quebec") from the balcony, giving new life to the secessionist movement and setting off a chill in Canada-France relations that lasted for years.

Decorative Flourishes – Noted art works in City Hall include the bronze *The Sower and Woman with Bucket* by Alfred Laliberté. A large bronze chandelier illuminates the main hall *(hall d'honneur)*. In the Council Chamber, stained-glass windows illustrate street scenes of Montreal in the 1920s.

Remnants of New France

The open space to the north of City Hall is a one-time military drill area called the Champs de Mars, now used for lunchtime breaks by office workers. The parallel ridges of stone that cut across the grass are all that remains of the wall that once surrounded the settlement. To the north you can see the gentle rise of land that forms part of the Montreal Escarpment, the ridge that runs the length of the island. Beyond is the skyline of downtown Montreal, the newer part of the city along Rue Sainte-Catherine that flourished in the latter part of the 19C.

Complexe Desjardins★

150 Rue Ste-Catherine Ouest. 514-845-4636. www.complexedesjardins.com. Open year-round Mon–Wed 9:30am–6pm, Thu–Fri 9:30am–9pm, Sat 9:30am–5pm, Sun noon–5pm (restaurants open every day 6 or 7am–8 or 9pm). Métro Place des Arts, green line.

When Complexe Desjardins opened in 1976, combining government offices and private enterprises, it immediately broke the mold. Gone are the long passageways of earlier underground centres. Complexe Desjardins revolves around a vast multi-storey interior cavern, diving down several levels below the street and soaring to cathedral heights. It's an indoor continuation of the terraces of Place des Arts across the way, and the activity—from shopping to rushing to a concert or multimedia presentation—is virtually non-stop. Enter through the doors on Rue Sainte-Catherine from the Métro, or if you're staying in the Hyatt Hotel, take the glass-sided elevator from upstairs into the cavern.

Counter-Complexe – Across Boulevard René Lévesque to the south is the federal government's counterpoint to the provincially owned Complexe Desjardins. **Complexe Guy-Favreau** is red brick on the outside, all utilitarian passageways on the inside and an assortment of federal offices upstairs in the six connected blocks. Together, Complexe Guy-Favreau, Place des Arts and Complexe Desjardins form an eastern suburb of Montreal's **Underground City** (see p 32).

Dominion Square Building★

1010 Rue Ste-Catherine. Métro Peel, green line.

Sparkling after a renovation and restoration, the Dominion Square Building, was an innovator at the time of its inauguration on the eve of the stock market crash of 1929. It follows Renaissance Revival stylistic dictates, with clearly defined top, middle and base sections. But for its height, the structure would blend into a Florentine streetscape.

In its details, however, this building was at the avant-garde of adapting to the extremes of the climate. Its insets brought natural light to offices inside, even on dreary days. The shopping arcade, protected from the extremes of weather, was a precursor of urban indoor malls.

Inside the Dominion

Go on, take a look inside. The ground floor of the Dominion Building houses the **Infotouriste Centre** *(514-873-2015)*, a one-stop public-private collaboration staffed with personnel ready to answer questions and provide maps and brochures. On-site vendors will arrange tours, car and bicycle rentals, sell guidebooks and otherwise see to your needs.

Dorchester Square★

Bounded by Rue Metcalfe, Rue Peel & Boul. René-Lévesque. Métro Peel, green line; or Bonaventure, orange line.

Dorchester Square is a green, leafy and pleasant expanse. With adjoining Place du Canada to the south, it forms the largest open area in Central Montreal. The one-time cemetery for cholera victims lies at the centre of what was once considered the dominant "Anglo" business area of Montreal, Quebec, and Canada. The park itself—called Dominion Square until a few years ago—tells Canadian history from a federalist viewpoint, which in Quebec is not the whole story.

The major thoroughfare bordering the south of the square was once named Dorchester Boulevard for Sir Guy Carleton, Lord Dorchester, the governor who secured the allegiance of French Canadians by protecting their land rights, religion and civil laws. The road now bears the name of René Lévesque, who as provincial leader sought to take Quebec out of Canada.

To the north, east and south stand some of the most impressive structures of the first half of the 20C in Canada.

Habitat '67★

2600 Ave. Pierre-Dupuis, Cité-du-Havre. http://cac.mcgill.ca/safdie/habitat.

Completed in time for the World Exposition of 1967, this remarkable "concept" apartment complex (in the manner of concept cars) was designed by young architect Moshe Safdie and constructed on the embankment that protects Montreal's port. Safdie took a page from the methods of automakers and had the apartment units fabricated on an assembly line. They were set into place at odd angles to form an open complex. Habitat is best viewed from the street in front of it that leads to St. Helen's Island; or from the Montreal waterfront.

One-Off – Unfortunately, Habitat proved to be unsuitable for the era of high energy prices that followed soon after its completion. But it did inspire others to go against the grain. It's not unusual to spot an apartment building in Montreal that's more pyramidal than rectangular. And right next to Habitat is **Tropiques Nord**, a more recent building with a greenhouse extending over the entire riverside exposure.

McGill University★

805 Rue Sherbrooke Ouest. 514-398-6555. www.mcgill.ca. Métro McGill, green line.

An oasis of lawns, trees and temples of learning, venerable McGill University occupies an enviable downtown campus, where Montreal slopes upward onto Mount Royal. The oldest university in Canada—consistently top-rated—was chartered by King George IV in 1821, with start-up funds provided by the estate of Glasgow-born fur trader James McGill. McGill now occupies 80 buildings spread across downtown and the MacDonald campus of agricultural studies at the western end of the island. About 30,000 students are enrolled.

Campus Walk – Start your stroll through the campus at the Roddick Gates on Rue Sherbrooke, erected in 1924. Walk up the central drive to appreciate the main buildings, named for illustrious teachers, alumni and benefactors, ranging from Peter Redpath to William Shatner of *Star Trek* fame. The **Redpath Museum★** *(see Museums)* stands to the west of the drive. At the far end, the **Arts Building** is the oldest on campus, the work of noted architect John Ostell.

Ritz-Carlton Hotel★

1228 Rue Sherbrooke Ouest. 514-842-4212. www.ritzcarlton.com. Métro Peel, green line.

Grande Dame of the Golden Square Mile—Montreal's Fifth Avenue—the Renaissance Revival Ritz opened in 1912, and has remained unchallenged as the epitome of elegance in the north. Take a quick look inside at the lobby paneled in dark wood, with leather banquettes and brass detailing. Or stay for lunch in the **Café de Paris**, or take high English tea in the **Jardin du Ritz** (Ritz Garden) with its signature duck pond.

Royal Bank of Canada★   *Banque Royale du Canada*

360 Rue St-Jacques Ouest. Open Mon–Fri 10am–4pm. Métro Place-d'Armes, orange line.

Montreal's skyline soared after 1924, when a height limit was repealed. The new Royal Bank headquarters was completed by 1928—just in time for the Crash of '29—with New York-style setbacks and traditional Renaissance tiers stretched to its full 20 storeys. The most pleasing part is the base, which could pass as a theatre itself. Indeed, it was modeled after the Teatro San Carlo in Naples. Pass through the polished brass doors under an ornate arched entry, into the lobby with its great arches, chandeliers, coffered ceiling and lively blue, pink and gilt décor.

The Underground City   *La Ville Souterraine*

Running beneath streets, threading between buildings, surfacing in multi-storied plazas diving way down to Métro level, is Montreal's Underground City, or RÉSO. Hotels, restaurants, rail stations, the suburban bus terminal, cinemas, nightclubs and even a library lie along the pedestrian network. There are busy thoroughfares and quiet corners, hubs of transportation and palaces of commerce. Over a quarter of a million people pass through each day.

As in the city above, the Underground has its neighbourhoods, ranging from upscale to workaday. Renovation is ongoing, along with controversy over designs. Trends at the beginning favoured keeping out the world above. More recently, light wells have pierced the netherworld.

The Underground City began with the passageways in and under Place Ville-Marie, completed in 1962. Tunnels snaked southward to join with Central Station. This is now the busiest neighbourhood and also one of the most attractive, with a cheery, village-like web of shops and sidewalk cafés.

As new exhibition centres and shopping areas opened, the Underground City extended its arms to welcome them: westward to Place Bonaventure and

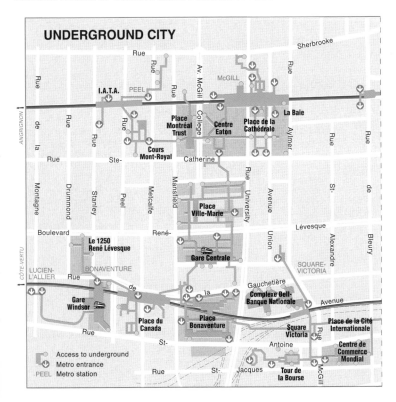

Windsor Station; northward to Les Cours Mont-Royal, Place Montréal Trust, the Eaton Centre and Promenades de la Cathédrale; and most recently, east beyond the Stock Exchange Tower and the Montreal World Trade Centre to the Palais des Congrès.

On a snowy day, you can enter the Underground City on the edge of Old Montreal and surface all the way up north at Rue Sherbrooke. And you can access your hotel, eat in fine restaurants, enjoy a movie or show and end the day without having once stepped outside.

As with above-ground towns, the success of the main axis has spurred rival developments. A second underground axis runs southward from Place des Arts to Complexe Desjardins, Complexe Guy-Favreau, and the Palais des Congrès (Convention Centre) south of Chinatown, then loops west to the original underworld. And a smaller but sophisticated rival consists largely of the passages running under and through the Université de Québec à Montréal campus around Rue Saint-Denis and Rue Sainte-Catherine. If past is prologue, these, too, will one day interconnect with the main network. Be sure to take along a map during your wanderings—the twists and turns can rival those of a medieval city, leaving you closer to your starting point than you meant to be.

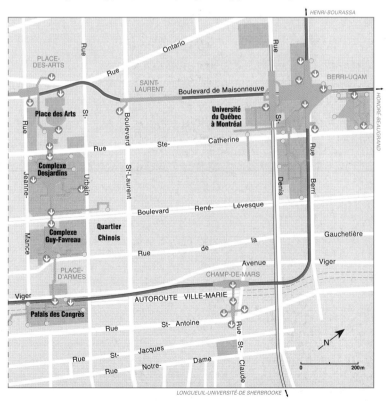

Sure there are ethnic enclaves like Chinatown and Little Italy, but Montreal's *quartiers* have twists you'll rarely find in North America. Travel back in time by strolling into Old Montreal, or explore public squares that are indoors. Find *chic* creations on Rue Saint-Denis and sleek fashions in Outremont. You'll even encounter Westmount, where English-speakers are a quaint ethnic group with their own peculiar customs. *Vive la difference!*

Old Montreal★★★   *Vieux-Montréal*

Stroll into the past in Old Montreal. Narrow cobblestone lanes, fieldstone colonial houses and convents, and early British commercial buildings were forsaken in the 19C as the business of Montreal, and its wealth, moved uphill. Today's innkeepers, shop owners and restaurateurs have turned the once-forlorn area into an open-air museum of days gone by.

Place d'Armes★

Bounded by Rue St-Jacques, Rue Notre Dame & Côte de la Place d'Armes.
Métro Place-d'Armes, orange line.

Under the French regime, all authority radiated from this urban square, laid out more than 300 years ago, reputedly on the site where Paul de Chomedey, Sieur de (sire of) Maisonneuve, skirmished with a native chieftain. A **monument★ [1]**

(see map on inside front cover) of **Maisonneuve** and key figures from his day stands at the centre.

To the south are the **Notre Dame Basilica★★★** *(see Landmarks)* and the **Old Sulpician Seminary★** *(see Historic Sites)*, seat of power for much of Montreal's history. On the north, the Bank of Montreal and the Royal Bank Building speak of Montreal's rising importance in the 19C and 20C. Down nearby lanes and alleys you'll find meditation gardens, green oases in the city, still owned by the Church.

Old City Walkabout

There's no better way to discover the charms of the old city than by following a whimsical course. Along the way, glimpse an old stone house in a court-yard through a coach entrance, find a shop full of surprises, or take a break at an inviting bistro. Hire a *calèche* for a tour at a clip-clop pace *(see Musts for Fun)*, or follow the suggested walking route on the next page.

Rue Saint-Jacques★

Montreal's Wall Street is diminished from its heyday, but remains an important financial centre. The **Bank of Montreal★** building on the north side of the Place d'Armes and the **Royal Bank of Canada★** are icons of the era of Montreal's financial ascendancy *(see Landmarks)*. The **Old Stock Exchange**, 453 Rue Saint-François-Xavier, a classical temple of a building, is now the **Centaur Theatre**. The new **Stock Exchange Tower★** *(Tour de la Bourse)* lies just to the west, at Victoria Square, across from the Montreal World Trade Centre.

Place Jacques-Cartier★★

Take wide, cobbled Place Jacques-Cartier from Rue Notre-Dame (east of Place d'Armes) down toward the port. What you see today dates from the heyday of English rule. The square's signature column is a **monument [2]** *(see map on inside front cover)* to Lord Horatio Nelson, victor of Trafalgar. Cafés and *terrasses* extend from sober stone buildings. Crowds and entertainers and flowers in bloom enliven the scene in mild weather. Just to the east are **Bonsecours Market★** *(see Must Shop)* and the **Chapel of Our Lady of Good Help★** *(see Historic Sites)*.

Rue Saint-Paul★★

Head a block up from the Old Port, and west along Rue Saint-Paul. Warehouses of old—mostly dating from the 19C—have been revived as boutiques and boutique hotels, ice cream shops and fine restaurants, galleries and clubs and, of course, souvenir shops.

Cruising the Neighbourhoods: Boat Trips from the Old Port★

Since Montreal began as a riverside settlement and still thrives as a port, a boat trip is a must. Most cruises depart from the Jacques Cartier Pier at the Old Port *(directly below Place Jacques-Cartier; Métro Champ-de-Mars, orange line)*.

- **Bâteau-Mouche** – 514-849-9952. www.bateau-mouche.com. May 15–Oct 15. Day cruise, $17.95 & up; dinner cruise $85. These Paris-style glassed-in "fly boats" ply the St. Lawrence River.

- **AML Cruises** – 514-842-9300. www.croisieresaml.com. Departs from Old Port mid-May–mid-Oct. $25–$160. AML operates sightseeing and dinner cruises; a river shuttle to Île Ste-Hélène or Longueuil ($4.50); and river and bicycle shuttle to Île Charron/Îles-de-Boucherville Park *(from Promenade Bellerive; Métro Honoré-Beaugrand, green line; $4)*. Cruises along the Lachine Canal operate in the vicinity of Atwater Market *(see Musts for Fun)*.

Plateau Mont-Royal★

North of Boul. St. Laurent. Métro St-Laurent (green line) or Sherbrooke (orange line).

To the north and east of Boulevard Saint-Laurent stretches Plateau Mont-Royal, a once-neglected neighbourhood where little brick houses are just the right size for urban pioneers, who have spruced up many of them with bright paint, sanded floors and modern wiring.

Boulevard Saint-Laurent

Above Rue Sherbrooke. Métro St-Laurent (green line) or Sherbrooke (orange line).

Locally known as The Main (as in Main Street), Boulevard Saint-Laurent is the traditional dividing line between French and English Montreal, where waves of immigrants first stopped. Landmarks include **Schwartz's Deli** *(3895 Boul. St-Laurent; see Must Eat)*, famous world-wide for Montreal smoked meat. As on upper Saint-Denis, low rents and large spaces have attracted entrepreneurs to former clothing factories and warehouses.

At all hours, The Main is alive with trendy bars (frequented by students from McGill University, to the west), and if there's a cuisine in the world that might find a local following, chances are that it's available somewhere on this street. As a shopping destination, The Main is a happy mix of upscale and downscale, with plenty of bargains still available in its unpretentious shops.

ex-Centris cinema complex – *3536 St-Laurent. See Performing Arts.*

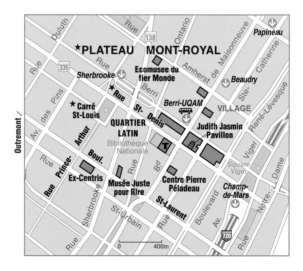

Rue Prince-Arthur

Turn east from Saint-Laurent onto Rue Prince-Arthur, named for a former governor-general and son of Queen Victoria. You're now on a onetime street of immigrants gone countercultural in the 1960s, and a little bit glitzy in the present. The asphalt has been lifted in favour of paving blocks, and pedestrians have the run of the former road, along with street performers, sidewalk artists and patrons of the sidewalk tables that overflow from restaurants up and down the way—where the cuisine of Greece prevails. By night, it's even busier as patrons flow in and out of bars, most especially the venerable **Café Campus** *(57 Rue Prince-Arthur Est)*.

Princely Lunch on a Pauper's Purse

The competition is fierce among the Greek restaurants along lively Rue Prince-Arthur, to everyone's benefit. **La Cabane Grecque** *(102 Rue Prince-Arthur Est; 514-849-0122)* is just one of numerous establishments that offer a soup-to-dessert meal for $12 at lunch and most evenings. Choose from moussaka, steak, roast chicken and shish kebab. The quality and quantity of food, considering the price, are surprising. And that's not all—most of the Rue Prince-Arthur establishments allow you to bring your own bottle of wine, which the waiter will uncork and serve at no additional charge. Stop in at the SAQ (liquor store) around the corner on Boulevard St-Laurent before you enter. Menus are posted at all the Greek restaurants along Prince-Arthur, allowing you to fine-tune your selection.

Carré St-Louis★

Continuing eastward, Rue Prince-Arthur is suddenly sedate as it ends at **St. Louis Square**, a garden with towering trees and a pavilion at its centre, surrounded by substantial 19C town houses with ornate detailing and decorative roofs. The greats of French-Canadian arts made their homes here, including poet Émile Nelligan, and secessionist sentiment is sometimes expressed through the display of the provincial flag. Take a break on one of the park benches before continuing eastward to Rue Saint-Denis *(see p 39)*.

The Old Port★   *Le Vieux-Port*

Rue de la Commune centred at Boul. St-Laurent. 514-496-7678.
www.quaysoftheoldport.com. Métro Place-d'Armes or Champ-de-Mars, orange line.

Down at the base of Place Jacques-Cartier, cross waterside Rue de la Commune, enter the garden and look toward the river and the piers of the Old Port. For centuries, canoes and ocean-going ships made it to this point on the St. Lawrence and no farther, stopped by rapids just around the bend. A few blocks toward the west is the restored entry to the Lachine Canal, which bypassed the rapids in 1825 and helped to make Montreal the second-busiest port on the continent.

Now, take a look behind. To the left and right spread buildings hardly changed in one hundred years, two-, three- and four-storeys tall, some clad in stone, others showing iron frames. Perhaps not a single one is architecturally "distinguished," but as a group, they bring a slice of an 18C port into the present day. Faded signs in English and French announce supply services; archways lead to former stables.

Port Revived – Cross the rail tracks (mostly unused) at any of a number of points into Montreal's Old Port itself, stretching 2.5km/1.5mi along the waterfront. Join the crowds on the great **esplanade** to enjoy the season, by motorized **tram**, rented bicycle, in-line skates, pedal boat, or ice skates. Attractions include the **Montreal Science Centre★** with its IMAX theatre, on King Edward Pier *(see Musts for Kids)*. Take a cruise *(see p 35)*, or climb the **Clock Tower** *(Tour de l'Horloge)*, erected in 1922 in memory of merchant sailors.

Look Out Below!

Roofs on homes in the Old Port and other areas are steeply pitched, in the absence of interior drains, to shed snow to the street below. If you're out in a dreamy winter cityscape after a heavy fall, watch out!

Rue Saint-Denis★ and the Latin Quarter
Quartier Latin

*Rue St-Denis between Rue Ste-Catherine & Rue Sherbrooke. www.quartierlatin.ca.
Métro Berri-UQAM or Sherbrooke, orange line.*

If Montreal's heart is at Place d'Armes, its French soul is in the Quartier Latin, along Rue Saint-Denis. Theatres, art movie houses and bookstores express the latest in *Québécois* culture. Cafes are thronged at all hours, in every season.

The Université de Montréal and the National Library of Quebec were established here to preserve and protect a language and culture perceived as imperiled in a continental sea of English—hence the nickname (as in the Latin Quarter area of Paris near La Sorbonne). Names, faces and buildings have changed, but the Latin Quarter remains a cultural capital of Quebec.

Rue Saint-Denis★

Stroll the *rue* and check out the myriad restaurants and boutiques. But there are sights to note, as well. The **Université de Québec à Montréal** (UQAM) occupies modern and heritage buildings along Saint-Denis *(south of Rue Ste-Catherine)*. **Théâtre St-Denis [T]** *(see map p 36)* showcases French-language singers, including Céline Dion.

Farther North – Above Rue Sherbrooke, and stretching onto side streets as far as Rue Duluth, lies the more avant-garde sector of St-Denis, where the studios, restaurants and boutiques of Quebec's up-and-coming fashion designers, chefs, jewellers, bakers, and even soap-makers crowd the wide sidewalks.

Joining In

You haven't truly experienced the Latin Quarter until you've lingered over an *apéro* (aperitif) or an espresso, while fellow patrons hunch over school texts, or debate the *question nationale* (secession or federation). Favourite places for a beverage are **Presse Café** *(1750 Rue St-Denis)*, and vegetarian **Le Commensal** *(1720 Rue St-Denis)*. Farther north, you can slyly gauge the hottest restaurants by the length of the line on Saturday night. **L'Academie** *(4051 Rue St-Denis at Duluth; 514-849-2249)*, with its low prices and Italian menu, rates high by this standard.

Chinatown★

Rue de la Gauchetière between Rue Côté & Boul. St-Laurent. Métro Place d'Armes.

You'll find all the elements of a North American Chinese quarter along pedestrians-only Rue de la Gauchetière, and in the blocks to the north and south: herbal shops, inexpensive wares from the People's Republic, exquisite lacquerware, pressed duck ready for carryout, a fortune-cookie factory, a Holiday Inn with a pagoda roof, and restaurants, restaurants, restaurants!

Montreal's Chinatown emerged in the 1860s, after railroad construction workers and mine laborers resettled in cities wherever the rails ran. In time, like other immigrants, the Chinese moved on into the larger society, but successive waves of immigrants have maintained the character of Montreal's Chinese quarter.

What To Do In Chinatown

Every excursion to Chinatown begins with a walk along **Rue de la Gauchetière**. Branch out to the busy intersecting streets lined with merchants, especially Boulevard St-Laurent and Rue Clark. The little park at la Gauchetière and Clark honors Sun Yat-Sen, first president of the Chinese Republic. The site of the first hand laundry, at St-Antoine and Jeanne-Mance, is something of a local landmark. The Holy Spirit Catholic Mission at 205 Rue de la Gauchetière holds an Oriental-style painting of the stations of the cross, and is a designated historic landmark.

Lunch for Less in Chinatown

Almost every visit to Chinatown includes a survey of menus posted in the windows of restaurants along Rue de la Gauchetière, and ends with tea and fortune cookies.

Feel like a hot-and-spicy Szechuan meal? **Jardin du Nord** *(80 Rue de la Gauchetière Ouest)* is a good choice for beef, chicken with walnuts, or crispy beef. The top price at lunch is just $12. Of course, spending is a personal choice, so if you require a lower outlay, look just next door at the **Guang Zhou**, where $6 buys soup and General Tao's chicken or Singapore noodles. And this is in the high-rent district along Chinatown's main street. Can prices go even lower? Look along Rue Clark and Rue St-Urbain to find the answer.

Outremont

On the eastern flank of Mont-Royal, south of Ave. du Parc and west of Boul. Mont-Royal. Métro Laurier, orange line, or Outremont, blue line.

What Westmount is to traditional English Montreal, Outremont is to French Montreal: well-off, well-educated, substantially constructed early in the 20C. Lawyers, doctors, politicians and teachers reside in Second Empire houses, though they only scale the lower reaches of the mountain, along Chemin Côte Sainte-Catherine.

Avenue Laurier

Outremontais (residents of Outremont) have their equivalent of Westmount's Greene Avenue. But Avenue Laurier offers a more varied selection of clothing boutiques, *pâtisseries*, cheese shops, and restaurants proposing refined cuisine. On Greene Avenue, a couple of restaurants set out chairs and tables in mild weather; in Outremont, the sidewalk cafés look as if they belong.

Avenue Bernard

Avenue Bernard, the other main shopping street of Outremont, is livelier and more avant-garde in its restaurants and boutiques. **Le Bilboquet**, at number 1311, serves its fabled ice cream in warm weather and cold. Restaurants here are known for sleek décor and arresting presentation, as well as good food.

Westmount

South of Rue Sherbrooke. Métro Atwater, green line, then two blocks west, or bus 24.

"English" in Montreal refers to anyone who speaks the language, regardless of background (*"anglophone,"* more accurately, in French). But the district of Westmount, a separate municipality with its own quirky ways, comes as close as you'll find to England itself.

Tea and English

A walk down **Greene Avenue** in Westmount reveals low-rise buildings housing a variety of shops that could just as well be in a well-off London suburb: book-stores, a toy shop, and restaurants where high tea is served every afternoon—except that signs are in French, as required by law.

Westmount's Tower

Just to the east of Greene Avenue is **Westmount Square★**, a landmark office and residential complex designed by Ludwig Mies van der Rohe. It extends downward into an exclusive shopping arcade that continues via underground passageway to the Plaza Alexis Nihon centre at the Atwater Métro station.

More of Westmount

For more English-Canadian flavour, continue westward along Sherbrooke, then follow Côte St-Antoine a couple of blocks to the lawn bowling green, where you'll see players garbed in whites from April onward. Farther West, at Sherbrooke and Melville, sits **Westmount Park**, with its updated centenary library and oh-so-English greenhouse.

A number of Montreal's museums are world-class, and some, such as the Canadian Centre for Architecture, have no peer anywhere. Others are off-beat or just plain fun. Perhaps best of all, the museum experience in Montreal is on a human scale. You can see a fair part of most collections in a few hours, and linger at items that interest you, without feeling rushed to see it all.

Contemporary Art Museum★★
Musée d'art contemporain de Montréal

185 Rue Ste-Catherine Ouest. 514-847-6226. www.macm.org. Open year-round Tue–Sun and holiday Mondays, 11am–6pm (Wed until 9pm). $8 (free Wed after 6pm). Métro Place-des-Arts, green line.

There's only one museum devoted exclusively to modern art (*art contemporain* in French) in all of Canada, and it's right here in Montreal. Everything in the building dates from 1939 and after.

The emphasis is on Canadian art, especially big-name Quebeckers. The likes of Jean-Paul Riopelle and Paul-Émile Borduas—some of whose works fall between Picasso and Native American symbolism—may be seen at times in Paris and London, but never in such concentration as in the *Musée d'art contemporain*.

This is no palace of dead painters. The permanent collection includes sculpture, photographs, prints and installations. The museum lives modern art by staging multimedia events, new dance, experimental theatre, contemporary music, video and film . . . and all this as a department of the provincial government—proof that Quebec is, indeed, different.

Almost an optical illusion shoehorned into a spare strip of land along one edge of the Place des Arts performance complex, the building manages to create ample and well-lit gallery space and a dramatic light-filled rotunda, a summer sculpture garden and even a sheltered walkway and colonnade on the stark Rue Jeanne-Mance side. Enter the museum from the east side or from the sheltered concourse of Place des Arts *(see Performing Arts)*.

Such a Deal

The **Montreal Museums Pass** provides entry to 32 city museums on three consecutive days for $35 ($45 with transit pass), including taxes. That amounts to the admission price at three major museums alone. The pass is available at most museum ticket counters and tourist information centres. Many museums also offer family rates for two adults and two children, as well as discounts for seniors, students and children.

McCord Museum★★   *Musée McCord*

690 Rue Sherbrooke Ouest. 514-398-7100. www.mccord-museum.qc.ca. Open year-round Tue–Fri 10am–6pm; weekends 10am–5pm; also holiday Mondays & July–Sept Mon 10am–5pm. $12. Métro McGill, green line, or bus 24.

The Collections – How did people dress 150 years ago during Montreal's winter? How did Native Canadians cook and sew and build? You'll find the answers in this wonderful collection of Quebec artifacts .

The McCord has everything from records of the fur trade to cartoons from modern Montreal newspapers. The permanent exhibit, **Simply Montreal,** selects from this treasure trove to present a portrait of how Montrealers have lived, eaten and played over the years. Daily life unfolds through dresses and formal outfits, hunting equipment, everyday objects from glassware to hoop skirts, and a sampling from a fabulous stock of period toys.

The Notman Archives – View ordinary, infamous and extraordinary Montrealers from over 100 years ago. Photographer William Notman immortalized them all on film over a period of 78 years, until his death in 1891.

Current Exhibitions – Materials selected from the museum's collection bring past and remote lives into the present. *Growing Up in Montreal* shows how the lives of children changed in the 20C. *Nuvisavik: "The Place Where We Weave"* delves into crafts as part of the culture of Baffin Island. Watch for an exhibition from the McCord coming to a museum near you.

Strolling Avenue McGill College

One of the shortest streets in Montreal, **Avenue McGill College** became one of the widest only a few years back simply to provide a dramatic approach to McGill University and a broad vista of Mount Royal. Such are priorities in Montreal, where appearances and *grandeur* count. Kiosks, display cases and public art adorn the broad sidewalks of the avenue, turning it into Montreal's greatest open-air museum. The most attention-getting piece is *The Illuminated Crowd*, a throng of comic-style humans molded in polymers by Raymond Mason, in front of no. 1981 Avenue McGill College. When it's not functioning as a thoroughfare, the avenue closes off easily at either end to become a plaza, or a handy setting for political demonstrations.

Montreal Museum of Archaeology and History★★
Musée d'archéologie et d'histoire de Montréal—Pointe-à-Callière

350 Place Royale at Rue de la Commune. 514-872-9150. www.pacmuseum.qc.ca. Open late Jun–Aug Mon–Fri 10am–6pm, weekends 11am–6pm. Rest of the year Mon–Fri 10am–5pm, weekends 11am–5pm. $12. Métro Place d'Armes, orange line.

If you think of history as dusty books and dustier costumes, think again. The Pointe-à-Callière museum manages to be futuristic and fascinating, while literally diving into the past. It's not only about history, it *is* history—located right where Samuel de Champlain established the first French trading post.

The striking **Éperon building**, the visible tip of the museum, faces the harbour; its railings, terraces and smooth surfaces are like the decks, hull and superstructure of a ship. A multimedia presentation—complete with actors, props, lights and sound effects—traces the history of Montreal, beginning with the Ice Age. The third-floor terrace and restaurant provide some of the best **views** of the port.

Archaeological Crypt – Head down from the main building to delve into history. Directly below Place Royale are the excavations of the original French trading post. It's all now stabilized, climate-controlled, lighted, and partially reconstructed. Visitors walk along the former bed of the Little St. Pierre River (later vaulted as the town sewer), through the first public square, and to the partially excavated remains of Montreal's first Christian cemetery. Sound and video are projected right onto the ruins to bring the old marketplace to life. Guided tours in English are offered on Saturdays, and museum personnel are always available to answer questions.

Old Customs House (l'Ancienne Douane) – The passageway through the crypt leads to the Old Customs House, completed in Neoclassical style in 1838 according to a design by John Ostell. The Customs House, emblematic of Montreal's importance as a British port, houses an exhibit on world trade, as well as the museum gift shop.

Montreal Museum of Fine Arts★★
Musée des Beaux-Arts de Montréal

1380 Rue Sherbrooke Ouest at Rue Crescent. 514-285-2000. www.mmfa.qc.ca. Open year-round Tue 11am–5pm, Wed–Fri 11am–9pm, weekends 10am-5pm. Closed Jan 1 & Dec 25. $15 (half-price Wed evening). Métro Guy-Concordia, green line, or bus 24.

The Fine Arts Museum is to Montreal what the Metropolitan is to New York—dignified, comprehensive, authoritative—but far more human in scale and presentation. A few hours here will give you an appreciation of the art of Canada and Quebec.

Hornstein Building – The original museum is a 1912 Beaux Arts monument faced in white marble. Beyond the colonnade and portico are a grand staircase and newer galleries in the Stewart Pavilion.

Canadian Collection – Pieces from French colonial days through the 20C are featured here. You'll see Inuit art, paintings by the Group of Seven, and works by Montrealers James Wilson Morrice, Ozias Leduc, and Alfred Laliberté.

Decorative Arts – A top drawing card is the collection of European and Canadian decorative arts. Holdings represent every major trend from Art Nouveau to post-Modernism.

Underground Museum – As a true Montreal institution, the museum plunges into passageways and halls that connect its two main buildings, right under Rue Sherbrooke. The **Galleries of Ancient Cultures** showcase masks and ritual objects from Africa and Oceania, porcelain from China, Indian sculpture, and pre-Columbian ceramics.

The Other Side of the Street: The Desmarais Building

On the south side of Rue Sherbrooke, the façade of the newer, contemporary section of the museum is a monumental sculpture in itself, the glass eye of a window set into a largely blank wall. Architect Moshe Safdie showed little respect for convention, blurring the borders between indoors and out with a soaring greenhouse foyer. But even masters make mistakes. The stairways, with ultra-short risers, are disorienting; keep to the elevators. Temporary exhibitions, along with works from the permanent collection, fill the huge, flexible spaces.

Biosphère★

160 Chemin Tour-de-l'Isle, Île Ste-Hélène. 514-283-5000. www.biosphere.ec.gc.ca. Open Jun–Sept daily 10am–6pm. Rest of year Mon & Wed–Fri noon–5pm; weekends, holidays and school breaks 10am–5pm including Tue. Closed Jan 1 & Dec 25–26. $9.50 ($15 with Stewart Museum). Métro Parc Jean-Drapeau, yellow line or Jacques-Cartier Bridge.

Once the United States pavilion at Expo '67, this wonder of modern architecture was reborn in 1995 as the Biosphère. Since then, it has reigned as the only museum on the continent devoted to water in general, and the Great Lakes and the St. Lawrence River in particular.

Inside the geodesic dome, the levels of the museum rise like the decks of a ship; an expanse of water lies directly below, and the St. Lawrence flows by on two sides—you're surrounded by the subject matter!

Water Wonders! – Dive into the topic as you walk on water using floating skates, construct watercourses, generate energy, follow the daily quest for survival, and design, steer, and even sink a ship. (Take a change of clothes.)

Planète Bucky – Sustainable development focuses on inventions of dome creator Buckminster Fuller, including the streamlined Dymaxion car, the Dymaxion house, and even the super-efficient Dymaxion bathroom, as well as the Biosphere's own wastewater-treatment marsh.

Specifics About the Sphere

- The geodesic dome is almost, but not quite, a sphere. In fact, it is two structures. The outer layer is made up of triangles, the inner of smaller hexagons.
- The dome rises to 62.8m/206ft and encloses 189,724 cu m/1,700,000sq ft.
- The frame is made of steel tubes welded to steel joints.
- The original dome was covered in (flammable!) acrylic panels.
- Constantly in touch with water, the newer museum is inspired by the river and laid out like a ship, with a hold, a bridge and a crow's nest.

Canadian Centre for Architecture★
Centre Canadien d'Architecture

1920 Rue Baile. 514-939-7026. www.cca.qc.ca. Open year-round Wed–Sun 10am–5pm (Thu until 9pm). $10 (free after 5:30pm Thu), including tour. Closed Jan 1 & Dec 25. Métro Guy-Concordia, green line.

Philanthropist, heiress, preservationist and architect, Phyllis Lambert practices what she preaches. When the derelict Shaughnessy House was about to be flattened, she stepped in with her chequebook and professional skills, and saw to its loving and painstaking restoration. The mansion became the centrepiece of a museum that celebrates public involvement in buildings and their design. Current exhibitions often focus on architecture from a specific era. CCA is also a research centre with an unparalleled collection of prints, drawings and photographs.

The Galleries – The new construction of CCA faces quiet Rue Baile with an imposing façade of granite and limestone. Despite the addition's mass, the galleries are relatively small-scale and interconnect in unpredictable ways.

Shaughnessy House– On the south side of the complex, this 1874 grande dame has been restored, adapted and updated, with new floors and recessed lighting that's effective, if not historically accurate. The mansion houses the conservatory—delightful on a sunny winter day—and the tearoom.

Sculpture Garden – Across busy Boulevard René-Lévesque, a plot of land isolated by expressway ramps is set with sculptures that suggest structures and elements of architecture, from an arcade that mirrors the Shaughnessy House to a homey oversized chair of a long-gone dwelling, literally elevated to prominence.

More Recycled Architecture

Take a break after your CCA visit in another example of Montreal architectural recycling of quite a different sort. **Le Faubourg Sainte-Catherine** (*1616 Rue Ste-Catherine Ouest; www.lefaubourg.com*) is a meeting of outlets of ready-to-eat exotic foods from the world over, along with specialty grocers and bakers, in an open-plan, multi-level indoor neighbourhood that was once an automobile showroom. Peek through the south windows to the heritage stone buildings of the convent of the Grey Nuns, some of which are not open to the public or even easily visible from the street.

Montreal History Centre★
Centre d'histoire de Montréal

335 Place d'Youville. 514-872-3207. www2.ville.montreal.qc.ca/chm.htm. Open Jan 10–Dec 10, Tue–Sun 10am–5pm. Closed Dec 11–Jan 9. $4.50. Métro Square-Victoria, orange line, or bus 61.

Even before you walk into the History Centre on Place d'Youville, you're in Montreal as it used to be. The Grey Nuns hospital *(Hôpital général des Sœurs Grises),* on the south side of Place d'Youville, traces its history to the 18C. Just down the street, the 1820 Bouthillier warehouses present an elegant cut-stone face, and rough fieldstone workaday buildings in the courtyard past the coach gate. The square itself housed the parliament of Canada—until rioters torched it in 1849.

Central Fire Station – The museum was once a fire station, but what a station! It was state-of-the-art for its day, with a drying tower just for hoses. Decked out in the Flemish style with decorative gable ends, the station has been a landmark from birth.

Permanent Exhibitions – **Montreal Five Times** takes you through the history of the city from the first fur trading post to the glory days of Expo '67 and the Olympics in the 1960s and 70s. Through images, special effects and objects, figures famous, infamous and ordinary tell their stories and re-create their times.

Montreal of a Thousand Faces is a personal visit with Montrealers from the present and recent past. Settle into a period living room, or eavesdrop in an old-style kitchen, then walk into a general store, an office where typewriters still clack, or the cloak-room of a factory. Video-taped testimonies recount lives and experiences.

Up on the Roof – You can even do what you're usually *not* supposed to do—climb up to the roof for a look around the neighbourhood from a daring perspective (it's quite safe here—in an enclosed greenhouse-style gallery).

Montreal's Offbeat and Special Museums

Every major city has an art museum or two, and probably some kind of science centre. But how many have a museum entirely devoted to insects? A radio heritage museum? A commemoration of the daily struggle in a poor neighbourhood? No matter where your interests lie, at least one of these is sure to be a must-see for you.

Château Dufresne★

2929 Rue Jeanne-d'Arc. 514-259-9201. www.chateaudufresne.qc.ca. Open year-round Thu–Sun 10am–5pm. $7. Métro Pie-IX, green line.

Once the home of the Decorative Arts Museum (now absorbed by the Museum of Fine Arts), Château Dufresne has returned to its roots and exhibits itself for itself. It is the fine private *hôtel* (town mansion) of the merchant-prince Dufresne brothers, modeled after the Petit Trianon at Versailles.

There's nothing modest about this family home. Massive Ionic columns mark the façade; high windows and balconies suit a milder climate. The bachelors Dufresne lived in separate wings decorated to their individual tastes—Marius, an architect and builder, favoured oak panelling, while Oscar, who owned a shoe factory, preferred mahogany and Italian marble. Period furniture and domestic objects decorate the château; all have been restored and located in their rightful places. Temporary exhibitions are also mounted.

The Fur Trade at Lachine National Historic Site★

Lieu historique national du Canada du Commerce-de-la-Fourrure-à-Lachine

1255 Boul. St-Joseph, Lachine. 514-637-7433. www.parcscanada. gc.ca/fourrure. $3.95. Open Apr–early Oct daily 9:30am–12:30pm & 1pm–5pm (weekends until 6pm); early Oct–Nov Wed–Sun 9:30am–12:30pm & 1pm–5pm. Closed Dec–Mar & Nov 11. Métro Angrignon, green line, then bus 195.

The tale of the fur trade, the business that made Montreal, is told in a venerable stone warehouse where pelts once arrived by river from the far reaches of the continent. Furs, fashion and speculation drove prices to dizzying heights and calamitous crashes, as you'll learn here. Combine a visit with a cycling trip westward from downtown along the **Lachine Canal** *(see Musts for Fun)*.

Marc-Aurèle Fortin Museum★   *Musée Marc-Aurèle-Fortin*

118 Rue St-Pierre. 514-845-6108. Open year-round Tue–Sun 11am–5pm. $5. Métro Square-Victoria, orange line.

The legacy of great artists tends to be thinly spread. But Marc-Aurèle Fortin's (1888–1970) status as a unique Quebec talent has made it possible to collect a significant number of his works in one place. Visit this museum and you'll appreciate Fortin's development over the years, and see Montreal and Quebec from his changing perspective.

Fortin aimed to paint rural Quebec landscapes without the conceits of European style. His innovative techniques included pre-coating canvases in black or gray *(manière noire)*, and pre-tinting sheets for watercolour, to lend a spongy texture to his work. The locale, a warehouse built in the 19C for the Grey Nuns, is itself worth the visit.

Redpath Museum of Natural History★
Musée d'histoire naturelle Redpath

859 Rue Sherbrooke Ouest, on the campus of McGill University. 514-398-4086. www.mcgill.ca/redpath. Open Mon–Fri 9am–5pm, Sun 1pm–5pm. Closed holidays. Métro McGill, green line, or bus 24.

Fossils, minerals and stuffed species from the far corners of the world, but especially from Canada and Quebec, fill the Redpath.

The ethnology collection contains 17,000 pieces from ancient Egypt, Equatorial Africa, Oceania, the Mediterranean and South America. Of course, no natural history museum worthy of the name can do without its dinosaurs and mummies, and you'll find those here, too. It's all in a lovely hall at McGill University, an unusual rounded classical temple with incongruous clerestory windows, a grand staircase, hardwood floors and wainscoting. The benefactor behind the building was Peter Redpath, whose name appears on most packaged sugar in Canada.

Écomusée du fier monde

2050 Rue Amherst. 514-528-8444. www.ecomusee.qc.ca. Open year-round Wed 11am–8pm, Thu & Fri 9:30am–5pm, weekends 10:30am–5pm. $6. Métro Berry-UQAM.

Once it was an Art Deco public bath—complete with arched portals, brass friezes and porthole windows—as well as a social centre, and the pride of a gritty neighbourhood where most lodgings had no baths or showers.

Today this people's museum commemorates the industrialization and de-industrialization of Montreal and the hardscrabble working-class life of the district's bygone inhabitants. The moving story of their daily life, celebrations, meeting places, and churches is told through photos, documents, and the surrounding buildings. Ask about the Sunday walking tours held in summer.

The Écomusée sits squarely in the Gay Village of today's Montreal. Huddled, tiny brick houses have been modernized with indoor plumbing, decorated with colourful paint, and gentrified with lovingly tended postage-stamp gardens—all quite a change from the not-so-glory days commemorated in the museum, and a wholly different *fier monde* (proud world).

Émile Berliner Radio Museum
Musée des Ondes Émile Berliner

1050 Rue Lacasse. 514-932-9663. www.berliner.montreal.museum. Open year-round Fri–Sun 2pm–5pm. $3. Métro Place Saint-Henri, orange line.

You listen to music on CDs and DVDs today, but it all began with the original gramophone invented by Émile Berliner. Flat records (recorded on one side only) and the Berliner Gramophone were first produced at a Montreal plant in 1900, and promoted using the trademark dog, Nipper. The company prospered, expanding into the most modern factory of its day in this industrial complex, and was eventually absorbed by RCA.

Antique gramophones are on display in a section of the onetime RCA Victor plant. Prize pieces include models fitted into fine cabinetry, Edison's wax cylinder machines and an RCA Victor Superheterodyne from 1935. Attendants will crank up the equipment so that you can appreciate state-of-the-art audio from a hundred years ago. Period advertisements tout the advantage of flat records over wax cylinders—a precursor of modern-day media wars.

Just For Laughs Museum   *Musée Juste pour rire*

2111 Boul. St-Laurent. 514-845-4000. musee.hahaha.com. Open year-round Thu–Sun by reservation only (minimum 15 persons). $9. Métro Saint-Laurent, green line.

Some citizens said there was nothing funny about spending tax dollars for a humour museum and others couldn't stop laughing. Was it worth the money? You be the judge. Whatever your conclusion, you'll have a one-of-a-kind experience. The humour museum is an outgrowth of the stunningly successful Just for Laughs festival *(see Calendar of Events)*, which has showcased numerous top comedians in their early days. If your language is English only, you'll probably not appreciate the presentations of Quebec humour. But you will relive the glory years of Buster Keaton (a Quebecker), Laurel and Hardy, Woody Allen, Johnny Carson, and other luminaries of the laugh. The cabaret upstairs is a venue for—what else?—comedy shows.

Montreal Planetarium   *Planétarium de Montréal*

1000 Rue St-Jacques West. 514-872-4530. www.planetarium.montreal.qc.ca. Hours vary seasonally. $8. Métro Bonaventure, orange line, or bus 107 on Rue Peel.

Stars rule! Montreal's planetarium (also known as the Dow Planetarium after the brewing family that brought it to life) is expectedly hemispherical on the outside. Inside, it's all state-of-the-art, with futuristic controls and sound system. Shows most days range from holiday and children's themes to Star Secrets and The Exotic Universe. English-language presentations alternate with French *(call or check Web site for schedules)*.

They range from grand forests in the city (Mount Royal Park), to minutely planned gardens (La Fontaine Park), to sedate surprises in busy neighbourhoods (Carré St-Louis), to reserves where raccoons and foxes share the wilderness with cross-country skiers (Cape St-Jacques Nature Park; *see Musts for Fun*). Whether you want to people-watch, take a break from the city, or indulge in solitary meditation, Montreal has just the park.

Montreal Botanical Garden★★
Jardin botanique de Montréal

4101 Rue Sherbrooke Est. 514-872-1400. www.ville.montreal.qc.ca/jardin. Open mid-May–mid-Sept daily 9am–6pm; mid-Sept–Oct 9am-9pm; Nov–mid-May Tue–Sun 9am–5pm (open holiday Mondays). Closed Jan 1 and Dec 24–25. Free guided tours daily except some Mondays 10am & 1:30pm (no tours in Oct). $12.75 mid-May–Oct 31, $9.75 winter, including Insectarium. Métro Viau, green line, then free shuttle, or bus 185.

Ranked among the world's finest horticultural facilities, Montreal's Botanical Garden holds over 22,000 species of plants, in 30 themed outdoor gardens, and protected in ten oversized greenhouses. And all this in a winter city!

In northern latitudes, keeping the flowers in bloom is important stuff. A recent director of the garden, Pierre Bourque, went on to become mayor of Montreal. His on-the-job diplomatic experience included negotiating the construction of the Chinese Garden, in concert with officials from the People's Republic of China.

Garden Highlights

Start at the reception garden. A mini-train tours the site from May–Oct.

- No visitor can miss the **Chinese Garden★**, the largest outside China. It's authentic, even in its moon gateway, imported boulders and pavilions re-assembled by workers from Shanghai.

- **Conservatories★** – The *serres d'exposition* follow geographical themes, from the Chinese greenhouse and "landscapes in pots" to a Mexican ranch, rain forest and tropical plantations.

- The stately **Japanese Garden** includes a bonsai collection, and emphasizes serenity and harmony through the interplay of plants, pebbles and water. Tea ceremonies are held in the pavilion.

- Local species and bonsais grow inside the **Tree House**, while the **First Nations Garden** emphasizes the relationship of the Inuit and Amerindians with their natural surroundings.

Mount Royal Park★★ *Parc du Mont-Royal*

*Voie Camillien-Houde & Chemin Remembrance, directly north of downtown.
514-843-8240. www.lemontroyal.qc.ca. Open year-round daily 6am–midnight. Walk up
Rue Peel, or Métro Mont-Royal, orange line, & bus 11.*

Mount Royal *is* Montreal, in name and in spirit. Urban life without its mass and greenery is unimaginable.

A great park covers the upper slopes and valleys of the mountain. Forests, a lake, playing fields, and jogging and bicycle trails are just steps from the centre of the city. If all this sounds like New York's Central Park, it's not by accident—both were designed by master landscape architect Frederick Law Olmstead.

But Mount Royal also has maple forests and lofty lookouts. In winter, skiers swish along cross-country trails on the flanks of the mountain, and up to and around the Cross, in their public, but very private, wood. Except for a single road (Voie Camillien-Houde/Chemin Remembrance), Mount Royal Park is closed to vehicles.

Best of the Park

Beaver Lake (*Lac aux Castors*), near the park's western edge, is deep enough for pedal boats in summer, and freezes quickly in winter to become a favourite skating rink (*see Musts for Fun*). The **ski lift** in the meadow beyond operates on weekends.

Smith House (*Maison Smith*), at the foot of an escarpment off the trans-verse road, is a venerable stone structure from 1858. Stop in to view the exhibit on the mountain's ecology, flora and fauna, and to warm up over a hot beverage and snack.

The **Chalet** is a more substantial stone building on the edge of the slope facing downtown, with a **lookout** (*belvédère*) and **views★★★** toward the Green Mountains of Vermont.

Illuminated at night, the 37m/120ft-high **Cross** (*follow the path from Smith House or the Chalet*) recalls a wooden cross erected in thanksgiving after Montreal was spared from a flood in 1643.

Camillien Houde Lookout faces the flatlands of eastern Montreal toward the Olympic Stadium and Montreal Tower.

Notre Dame Island★   *Île Notre-Dame*

Access via Pont de la Concorde (Concorde Bridge).

This former embankment along the St. Lawrence Seaway was expanded with fill from excavations for Montreal's Métro (subway), just in time for Expo '67, the 1967 World's Fair. A bridge joins it with St. Helen's Island (although there is often no vehicular access from one to the other).

Island Sports

The pavements give way to the **Montreal Grand Prix** automobile race in June, and the **NASCAR Busch Series** in August. At other times, the **Circuit Gilles-Villeneuve** track hums with inline skates. The **Olympic Basin** has hosted rowing competitions since 1976.

The Principal attraction is the **Montreal Casino** *(see Musts for Fun)*, the former French pavilion at Expo '67, which resembles a foreshortened ship. At the western end of the island, the **beach** encircles an artificial lake, filled with St. Lawrence River water that is largely cleansed by the plants in an adjacent lagoon.

Flower Power – An international gardening competition, the **Floralies**, was once held on Notre Dame Island—and never closed. One of Montreal's more enchanting surprises, it displays exotic gardens with regional themes, planted along a series of canals.

St. Helen's Island★   *Île Ste-Hélène*

Access via Pont Jacques-Cartier (Jacques-Cartier Bridge). Automobiles are directed to parking lots on Île Ste-Hélène; through traffic to the Concorde Bridge may be restricted.

This former military outpost sports a **marina** and **lake** at the eastern tip, site of a spectacular fireworks competition on summer weekends. Quebec's most modern outdoor pools, built for the 2005 World Aquatic Championships, invite swimmers, and a forest with a pond and falls offers seclusion. Most significant among the public works of art here is *Man*, by **Alexander Calder**. In January, Montreal's **Winter Carnival** *(Fête des Neiges)* takes over the island *(see Musts for Fun)*.

Also here are the **Old Fort** and **Stewart Museum★** *(see Historic Sites)*, the **Biosphère★** *(see Museums)* and **La Ronde★** amusement park *(See Musts for Kids)*.

Jean Drapeau Park   *Parc Jean-Drapeau*

Île Ste-Hélène and Île Notre-Dame. Access via Pont de la Concorde (Concorde Bridge) or Pont Jacques-Cartier (Jacques Cartier Bridge). 514-872-6120. www.parcjeandrapeau.com. Open year-round daily 6am–midnight. Métro Jean-Drapeau, yellow line, then bus 167 around the park; or by bicycle or by boat from the Old Port.

It's only a single subway stop from downtown, but Jean Drapeau Park is, as they say, a world away. It hosted the entire world as the site of the Expo '67 fair, and Montrealers still enjoy the facilities left behind—the Biosphère, Montreal Casino and La Ronde amusement park—to this day.

La Fontaine Park   *Parc La Fontaine*

North of Rue Sherbrooke, between Ave. du Parc-La Fontaine & Ave. Papineau. Open daily 6am–midnight. Métro Sherbrooke, orange line, or bus 24.

Meticulously planned, La Fontaine Park is an integral part of the urban fabric. Whereas the trails and paths of Mount Royal follow natural contours, the pavements of La Fontaine are geometrically inspired. Whereas Mount Royal is largely wild, La Fontaine is planted to display colours throughout the milder months.

Pedal boats are available for rent, and in winter, the pond becomes a skating rink. Cross-country skiers find enough terrain for a workout here, and the Théâtre de Verdure is Montreal's favourite outdoor performance venue. Most of the shows are free, including ballet, classical music and drama in French and English *(details at Centre Infotouriste; Dorchester Square, behind 1010 Rue Ste-Catherine Ouest, or call 514-873-2015; see Performing Arts)*.

Best Views in Montreal

Montreal's topography encourages looking up, over and down on the city. Here are Montreal's must-view points, in parks, towers and hidden aeries:

Mount Royal Park★★ – The forest in the city has *two* leading viewpoints. The **Chalet Lookout** *(Belvédère du Chalet)* reveals a fabulous **view★★★** of all of downtown, and the river and mountains beyond. **Camillien Houde Lookout** *(Belvédère Camillien-Houde)* features a **view★★** of Montreal Tower and Olympic Stadium.

Avenue McGill College – Gaze straight up one of the widest streets downtown, toward the greenery of McGill University, and, beyond it, the forest of Mount Royal.

The Montreal Tower – This 175m/574ft-tall leaning tower provides a thrill on the way up, and spectacular **views★★★** of the city from the top.

Port Panorama – Climb to the outside terrace of the **Montreal Museum of Archaeology and History★★** *(350 Place Royale; see Museums)* for a **view★** of the waterfront or head to the terrace bar atop the Auberge du Vieux Port, 97 Rue de la Commune Est . On Clock Tower pier, trek the 192 steps inside the **clock tower** itself. Or climb the tower of the **Chapel of Our Lady of Good Help★** *(Chapelle Notre-Dame-de-Bon-Secours)* for the highest viewpoint accessible in Old Montreal *(see Historic Sites)*.

Revolving Courses – For dinner with an ever-changing outlook, head to the rooftop **La Tour de Ville** restaurant of the Delta Centre-Ville Hotel *(777 Rue University; see Must Eat)*.

Westmount Summit Lookout – The mansions of one of the wealthiest neighbourhoods in Canada are in the foreground of your **view★** to the St. Lawrence from the summit of Westmount *(take bus 166 on Chemin Côte-des-Neiges, then walk up Chemin Belvédère to Summit Circle)*.

With almost 400 years behind it since the French settled, and a people who are as proud of their past as of their present, Montreal packs a historical punch hard to equal on this side of the ocean. Turn a corner downtown, and you'll come across a church that's been filled with hymns for centuries; a humble stone residence with a steep roof that has shed snow through hundreds of winters; the town home where a bourgeois family dwelled before there were fashionable suburbs; or a quiet ecclesiastical garden now surrounded by skyscrapers.

Bonsecours Market★   *Marché Bonsecours*

350 Rue St-Paul Est, along the waterfront. 514-872-7730. www.marchebonsecours.qc.ca. Open Jun–Aug daily, 10am–9pm; Apr–May Sat–Wed 10am–6pm, Thu & Fri 10am–9pm; Labor Day–Oct Sun–Wed 10am–6pm, Thu–Sat 10am–9pm; Jan–Mar 10am–6pm. Exhibition hall hours vary. Métro Champ-de-Mars, orange line.

Standing above the rooftops of **Old Montreal★★★**, the central silvery dome of Bonsecours Market bespeaks power and purpose well beyond its function as a humble market. When viewed from the water, the cut-stone façade, with its oversized windows and columned portico, is as grand as a palace in Venice.

Bonsecours has, indeed, been more than a market. It began as a place for the exchange of goods in 1847, replacing the outdoor markets subject to inclemency on Place Jacques-Cartier. The plan of builder William Footner was to impress all with the "overwhelming image of the beauty and importance of the flourishing City of Montreal." Over the years, the Greek Revival-style building morphed into Montreal's city hall, a concert auditorium, and, for a time, became the seat of the parliament of United Canada, after the legislature on Place d'Youville was torched in the rioting of 1849. It also remained the city's premier farmers' market until 1963. With its former grandeur now restored, the market comprises a collection of upscale boutiques tucked into nooks along the great galleries *(see Must Shop)*.

Maison du Calvet★

401 Rue Bonsecours. 514-282-1725. www.pierreducalvet.ca. Métro Champ-de-Mars, orange line.

One of the more notable homes that remains from the French *régime* once belonged to Pierre du Calvet. A noncomformist in every way, he was a merchant in a colony of priests and farmers, a Protestant among Catholics, a supporter of the British against the French, and later of the revolutionary Americans against the British. His residence was erected in 1725 at the northeast corner of the intersection of Rue St-Paul with Rue Bonsecours. The house of Pierre du Calvet now shines as an elegant hotel. Walk in and take a look at massive fieldstone walls and the beamed ceilings.

Château Ramezay★

280 Rue Notre-Dame Est. 514-861-3708. www.chateauramezay.qc.ca. Open Jun–Sept daily 10am–6pm; Oct–May Tue–Sun 10am–4:30pm. $8. Métro Champ-de-Mars, orange line.

Though far from the *métropole*, the administrators of New France made few concessions to their wild surroundings. You can see it in Governor Claude de Ramezay's mansion, completed in 1705. While other buildings huddled along narrow lanes, the governor's great stone residence stood on an expansive estate.

The new British overlords took over the premises after the Conquest (known in French to this day as *La Défaite*, The Defeat). Invading American Revolutionaries set up headquarters here in 1775, and Benjamin Franklin was offered the entertainments of the house.

Château Ramezay was expanded over the years, and remodeled to create huge vaulted spaces. The original kitchens and service areas remain. An oddity is the antique mahogany paneling in the Salle de Nantes, which found its way here in the 20C. It originally graced the headquarters of the French West India Company, which once owned the property.

Museum – Pieces on display—Native artifacts, clothing, letters, tools— illustrate life on Montreal island, when survival of the community depended on the goodwill of Amerindians, unsteady supply lines, and adaptation to an unforgiving winter. Be sure to see the collection of early Canadian paintings from the 18C and 19C. Recorded music and personnel in period costumes help to re-create entertainment among the highborn, and the daily round of chores for those who served them.

Café and Gardens – You'll be as privileged as the governor of yore to avail yourself of his gardens in mild weather, with the additional amenity of a contemporary café. This replanting is practical as well as attractive. It includes a kitchen garden (*potagerie*) and orchard as well as plants for decoration, and a border of herbs and medicinal plants. Entry to the gardens is free.

Chapel of Our Lady of Good Help★
Chapelle Notre-Dame-de-Bon-Secours

400 Rue St-Paul Est. 514-282-8670. www.marguerite-bourgeoys.com. Open May–Oct Tue–Sun 10am–5:30pm, Nov–mid-Jan & Mar–Apr Tue–Sun 11am–3:30pm. Closed mid-Jan–Feb. $6 (free entry to chapel). Métro Champ-de-Mars, orange line.

Montrealers are fond of Bon-Secours Chapel. Because it's the church of the much-loved Sister Marguerite Bourgeoys, and the favourite chapel of sailors, moves to demolish the church have always been defeated. The current Bon-Secours Chapel was constructed starting in 1771, directly over the foundations of the first stone church in Montreal. It has the typically tall steeple of a country church, sheathed in copper. Inside, Bon-Secours radiates humility. Its notable decorations are not gilt altarpieces, but late-19C paintings on fitted boards of wood. Carved ships, gifts from sailors, hang in the sanctuary.

Museum – Marguerite Bourgeoys (1620–1700) founded the original church and school on the site. Born into prosperity, she gave up her worldly advantages to become the first teacher on the island. She established the Congregation of Notre Dame, the first order of nuns in the Americas to minister to the community outside the cloister. Former classrooms and parts of the tower make up the museum devoted to her works and memory. Her story is partly told through doll-like figures in a series of vignettes. Marguerite was elevated to sainthood in 1982.

Above and Below

While you're exploring the church, climb the stairway to the tower, completed in 1894 as the base of the 9m/30ft statue of the Virgin Mary with arms stretched toward the river. The upper terrace offers one of the best and highest **panoramas**★ of Old Montreal, and of the St. Lawrence River and its islands.

Then descend below the nave, and back into time. Excavations have revealed the foundations of the original stone church, wooden posts from colonial fortifications, charred remains from the 1754 fire that destroyed the original church, and signs of an aboriginal settlement, perhaps more than 2,000 years old.

The Old Fort and Stewart Museum★

20 Chemin Tour-de-l'Île, Île Ste-Hélène. 514-861-6701. www.stewart-museum.org. Open year-round mid-May–mid-Oct daily 10am–5pm. Rest of the year Wed–Mon 10am–5pm. Closed Jan 1 & Dec 25. $10. Métro Jean-Drapeau, yellow line, then bus 167.

Old Fort *(Vieux-Fort)* – British authorities decided to fortify Montreal, and with good reason. The rebellious Americans had occupied the city in 1775, and the young nation had invaded Canada in 1812. The colonial government acquired St. Helen's Island in 1818 and began construction of defenses. Eventually, the American threat eased, and the fort was abandoned.

Stewart Museum★ *(Musée David M. Stewart)* – Located in the Old Fort, the museum was founded in 1955 by philanthropist David M. Stewart (1920–1984), heir to the MacDonald Tobacco fortune. Exhibits here tell the story of the two European powers that clashed in North America, and of military campaigns in Canada, from the American invasions of 1775 and 1812 to the *Patriote* rebellion of 1837 and expeditions to the Pacific. There are weapons, maritime instruments, maps and

documents, to be sure, and complete military uniforms from early in the 19C, as well as all the utensils and instruments used to prepare food and to light dwellings.

History Lives

The power of the fort's tale lies in the telling. Throughout the summer, troops of the Olde 78th Fraser Highlanders and the Compagnie franche de la Marine drill and prepare for battle, while keeping a wary eye on each other. The Highlanders, in Tartan kilts, break the monotony of garrison duty with dances performed to the skirl of bagpipes. Maneuvers take place daily at 11am, parades at 3 and 4:30pm. The 1pm salute by the 24-pounder Bloomfield gun can be heard on Mount Royal. *Reenactments are held daily late Jun–late Aug. Call or check online for latest schedules.*

Old Sulpician Seminary★
Vieux Séminaire de Saint-Sulpice

130 Rue Notre-Dame Ouest. Métro Place d'Armes, orange line.

On Place d'Armes next to the **Notre Dame Basilica★★★** *(see Landmarks)*, the Vieux Séminaire is the oldest building standing on the island of Montreal. It was completed for the Sulpician order in 1687, when running a religious brotherhood meant a lot more than quietly serving God.

The Order – Founded in Paris by Jean-Jacques Olier in 1641, the Sulpician Order was firmly rooted in Montreal by the mid-17C. The Sulpicians acquired the mission of Ville-Marie in 1663—a sort of franchise that made them feudal masters of the island of Montreal for more than 200 years, entrusted by the king with maintaining the good order of his properties and of the people who occupied them.

The Seminary – The Sulpicians were already well established in New France by the time construction started on their seminary. Of course, as secular powers, they sited their base of operations on Place d'Armes, the very centre of authority.

Rough stonework, dormers, and the relatively steep roof to shed snow are characteristic of early Quebec buildings that take advantage of local materials. But this is a classical building in local garb. The pediments, inset columns, and orientation around an open courtyard—not the best solution for Montreal's chilly climate—were transplanted directly from France.

The premises expanded with the order; the main building was enlarged in 1704 and 1712, and the courtyard wings were added. Today the building continues to serve as a residence for the Sulpician Order.

Seminary Clock – Set into the seminary roof, the clock dates from 1701, which makes it one of the oldest anywhere in the United States and Canada. Oddly, its wooden mechanism survived until 1966, when it was replaced with modern electrical workings.

Sir George-Étienne Cartier National Historic Site★
Lieu historique national du Canada de Sir George-Étienne Cartier

458 Rue Notre-Dame Est. 514-283-2282. www.pc.gc.ca/cartier. Open late May–Aug daily 10am–6pm. Apr–late May & Sept–late Dec Wed–Sun 10am–noon & 1pm–5pm. Closed Jan–Mar. $4 ($6 with seasonal reenactments, call or consult Web site for schedule). Métro Champ-de-Mars, orange line, or bus 14.

If any man embodies the struggle to make Canada, it's George-Étienne Cartier. Born in a small town in 1814, he started his public life by taking up arms, and had to flee after the failed 1837 Patriote rebellion. But back he came, to achieve by peaceful methods what he couldn't accomplish with a gun: representative government with a place for French Canadians, both in their home region and in Ottawa. The ex-rebel ended up Sir George-Étienne, knighted by Queen Victoria. He helped establish the spirit of compromise and tolerance that would come to characterize political dialogue in Canada; today he is venerated as a civil hero, one of the Fathers of Confederation.

Life and Times of Sir George-Étienne

Reenactments here highlight the lives of the famous and the less so in the times of Cartier. Have a taste of the old art of fine living, when the leisure class made its own entertainment using the piano in the salon, and servants (all apparently still in the employ of the house, in this case) scurried about to please owner and guests. The interiors are the height of refined elegance of the time, with gold-leaf molding and plush wallpaper. Sound effects, from a steam engine to church bells, echo the street music of the day. Oversized photos reproduce downtown scenes, and mannequins display the outfits of Victorian Montrealers. Upstairs, the focus is on Sir George-Étienne Cartier (1814–1873), first as a lawyer and businessman, and later, as cabinet minister.

The Buildings – The Cartier property consists of two adjoining homes used in different periods by the family. On the street side they're built in an early version of the Second Empire style, with gables and pitched sections of roof at the top, and imposing cut-stone facing. Yet the rear exposure, in rough fieldstone, is deeply rooted in traditional Quebec. The buildings and the rooms have been restored to re-create the days when Cartier lived here.

Historic Sites in the 21st Century

What to do with a stately convent that's no longer in use but occupies valuable property? A heritage church that has lost its congregation? A stately hotel that's long on charm but short on modern amenities?

Why knock it down when you can stabilize it, clean it, re-wire it, and build a new building under and around it while preserving the beauty of times gone by and contributing to the ambience of the city? Not to mention making a profit.

In Montreal, what goes up doesn't have to come down. It's part of living in the present with grace and traditions that elsewhere are in the past. Here are some examples:

Christ Church Cathedral★

1444 Ave. Union at Rue Ste-Catherine. 514-843-6577. www.montreal.anglican.org/cathedral. Open year-round daily 10am–5pm & for services. Métro McGill, green line.

On the surface, Christ Church Cathedral appears much as it always has. The landmark Anglican church of Montreal, designed by Frank Wills and built of limestone, was completed in 1859 to serve the elite of its day. But a declining congregation led to financial straits; in addition, the church was literally sinking.

The solution was to lease the land to the north of, and *under* the landmark for commercial development. For several years, the cathedral sat perched in the air on concrete piers while the **Promenades de la Cathédrale** shopping complex was excavated beneath, and the office tower now known as **Tour KPMG★** was erected to the north, mirroring the church in its polished aluminum surface, cavernous lobby, and peaked roof.

The neo-Gothic cathedral is now as glorious as ever, famed for its organ and choirs. Note the carved stone above the arches, depicting the foliage of Mount Royal. The Coventry Cross is made of nails from the bombed-out cathedral in Coventry, England, and the stone screen behind the altar is a World War I memorial, engraved with scenes from the life of Jesus. If you're not familiar with the spire, you'll do a double take. No, it's not stone, at least not any more. The weighty 1927 original, added to inadequate underpinnings, caused the whole church to sink. It was replaced in 1940 with this faux-stone spire made of lightweight aluminum.

Maison Alcan★

1188 Rue Sherbrooke Ouest. Open year-round daily, 7am–midnight. Métro Peel, green line.

Can a modern aluminum skyscraper co-exist with a hotel that has seen better days? In the same neighbourhood? On the same site? Evidently so. Maison Alcan (Alcan House) is a showcase not only of aluminum as a beautiful building material, but one in harmony with the former hotel and adjacent town homes that it envelops. Daring in its use at the time (1983), aluminum has become the sheathing of choice in modern, energy-saving buildings in Montreal, covering layers of insulation and mimicking windows where there are none. Along similar lines is the **Banque Nationale de Paris★** (**BNP**), a few blocks away on Avenue McGill College near Sherbrooke, which envelops a row of elegant greystone town houses that would otherwise have been demolished.

The Windsor★

1170 Rue Peel. Métro Peel, green line.

The elegant Windsor Hotel of 1878 lost its main wing to fire in 1957, and the CIBC Tower went up on thè site. Until 1981 the hotel functioned in what remained—an outsized mansion with a huge mansard roof relieved by dormers and rounded windows. It lives once again in the restored splendour of suites occupied by today's business giants. Unfortunately, the ornate interior atrium is not open to the public.

Dawson College

3040 Rue Sherbrooke Ouest. www.dawsoncollege.qc.ca. Open year-round Mon–Sat. Closed Sun & school holidays. Métro Atwater, green line.

Former Mother House of the Congregation of Notre Dame, Dawson College occupied a prime piece of underutilized real estate on the western edge of downtown. The facilities of a junior college were scattered in several buildings in an industrial area down the hill. In 1998, after extensive renovations, the two were joined, with new facilities built largely into the ground.

Judith Jasmin Pavillon, Université de Québec à Montréal

405 Rue Ste-Catherine Est at Berri. Métro Berri-UQAM.

The entire Saint Jacques Church was not saved when the University of Quebec expanded its Montreal downtown campus between 1976 and 1979, but the lovely Gothic façade on Rue Berri was salvaged, along with the bell tower and transept. The abbreviated church is further reflected in the arched passageways of the new building.

For thrills, chills, and adventure with flair, you've come to the right place! Indoors or out, winter or summer, active or relaxed, opportunities for fun abound in every season.

Calèche Ride in Old Montreal★★

Place d'Armes or Rue de la Commune, Old Montreal. Métro Place-d'Armes. $45/30min, $75/hr.

The best conveyance along the romantic streets of **Old Montreal★★★** is a horse-drawn carriage, straight out of the 19C. The best place to hire one is by Notre Dame Cathedral or at the Old Port. The best day for a carriage ride is Sunday, in the morning, when most motorized traffic has disappeared. The best season is any season—in the warmth of summer, under the crisp autumnal sun, or snug under blankets in January.

Travel the Lachine Canal★★

From the Old Port to the borough of Lachine. 514-283-6054. www.pc.gc.ca/lhn-nhs/qc/ canallachine. Open year-round daily dawn–11pm; full services available mid-May–mid-Oct. Métro Square-Victoria, orange line (Old Port) or Métro Lionel-Groulx & bus 191 (Lachine).

Pedal, ski or ride a boat through history along the Lachine Canal. It's your choice and the season's whim, as to how you'll discover the historic waterway. The retired canal's been spruced up since its working days with a biking and ski trail, picnic tables and landscaping. Along this National Historic Site, the worn brick hulks with hardwood innards have been reborn as condos. And, more recently, the locks and bridges have been repaired and upgraded.

On Two Wheels – Rent a bicycle at Montreal's Old Port and pedal into the past along the banks of the Lachine Canal. The route winds gently down, then back up at passenger and pedestrian bridges that link the two banks, and crosses the restored lock gates.

Atwater Market

Corner of Rue Atwater & Rue Notre-Dame Ouest. 514-937-7754. www.marchespublics-mtl.com. Métro Lionel-Groulx.

The place where Montrealers shop and sip beverages in the continental manner, Atwater Market is an excellent stopping point. Refresh yourself with a cappuccino and a snack from the cornucopia of produce and imported gourmet items at this indoor-outdoor market. To the west, the poplar-shaded bicycle trail traces the towpath where workhorses once trod.

Lachine Canal Crossroads – Twelve kilometers out, you'll come back to the St. Lawrence at the Lachine entrance. Stop at the **Lachine Canal Visitors' Centre**, straight ahead between the two locks, where outdoor signs explain the evolution of the canal. The **Lachine Museum**, just to the south, holds a charming collection of local artifacts and miniature trains *(1 chemin du Musée; 514-634-3478; http://lachine.ville.montreal.qc.ca/musee; open Apr–Dec Wed–Sun 11:30am–4:30pm)*. Along the north side of the canal entrance, the bicycle trail continues past the **Fur Trade at Lachine National Historic Site** *(see Museums)*.

Going Home – For more discoveries, return along Boulevard LaSalle and the St. Lawrence River. **Rapids Park** *(Parc des Rapides)*, five kilometers out, is an unexpected haven of water birds in a restored marsh and the closest you'll get to the Lachine Rapids without going over them in a raft *(514-367-6351; www.poledesrapides.com)*.

On the Water – Most Montreal **harbour cruises★** poke into the restored lock at the eastern end of the canal before heading back out to the main channel of the river. A more leisurely cruise is available near Atwater Market. *For information, contact:* Lachine Canal Historic Cruise *(Croisière historique sur le Canal de Lachine)*, *Lachine Canal near Atwater; 514-846-0428; www.croisiere canaldelachine.ca; May 20–Oct 10; $16.75; Métro Lionel-Groulx.* Kayaks can also be rented seasonally in the same area *($15–$25/hr; 514-842-1306)*.

Jet Boating and Rafting★★

Jet Boating Montreal, Old Port, Clock Tower Pier. 514-284-9607. www.jetboatingmontreal.com. May–Oct. $60 adults, $40 children. Powered ride where pioneers feared to paddle, and rafting, too. Métro Champ-de-Mars.

Rafting Montreal, 8912 Boul. LaSalle. 514-767-2230. www.raftingmontreal.com. May–Sept. $40 adults, $23 children rafting; $48 adults, $28 children jet boating in the rapids. Free shuttles run from the Infotouriste Centre (tourist office), 1010 Rue Ste-Catherine Ouest. Métro Angrignon, green line, then bus 110.

You're floating down a tranquil river one minute, and in a roiling, drenching contest with Mother Nature the next. You soak in rays of sunlight, and suddenly you're soaked in water. You're not in the wilds of Colorado, but on the St. Lawrence in Montreal. Challenge  the Lachine Rapids in a jet boat, or under your own steam in a raft. It's as much fun as a remote river trip, at a much lower price.

Try Your Luck At Montreal Casino

Île Notre-Dame. Access via Pont de la Concorde (Concorde Bridge). 514-392-2746. www.casinos-quebec.com. Open year-round daily 24hrs. Patrons must be at least 18 years old. Métro Jean-Drapeau, yellow line, & bus 167 or free shuttle from Dorchester Square.

Montreal's casino is proof that sometimes governments get it right. The casino has had to expand several times since opening in 1992. Currently, it houses more than 3,000 slot machines and 120 gaming tables, not to mention a night-club, and a range of restaurants from gourmet to moderate.

Games – Aside from craps, all major games are offered, including black-jack, slot machines, keno, poker, roulette, and mini, midi and grand baccarat.

Dress Code – The casino enforces a dress code, more relaxed than it used to be, but it prohibits bare feet, motorcycle boots and cutoffs. And the drinks are *not* free.

Extras – Lottery and gambling win-nings go untaxed in Quebec. The house cut is claimed to be lower than that in Las Vegas, Atlantic City and Detroit. Parking is free.

The Building – Montreal Casino now occupies the French pavilion of the 1967 World's Fair and the adjacent Quebec pavilion. Unlike most gambling halls, it has windows, revealing spectacular views of the Montreal skyline and the St. Lawrence River.

Skating Outdoors . . .

Bring your skates or rent them on-site to enjoy a quintessential Montreal experience in winter. Neighbourhood indoor rinks open in October, and out-door rinks of natural ice are maintained in many parks throughout the winter. Here are a couple of choice spots to strap on skates:

Beaver Lake in Mount Royal Park★★ *Lac au Castors*

Take Voie Camillien-Houde or Chemin Remembrance to the parking areas. Paid parking at Beaver Lake. 514-843-8240. www.lemontroyal.qc.ca. Park open year-round daily 6am–midnight. Métro Mont-Royal, orange line, & bus 11, or bus 166 & bus 11.

Shallow Beaver Lake freezes quickly once winter sets in. There's no formality and there are no fees here. When you get cold, you can always pop into the adjacent pavilion to warm up.

Old Port★   *Vieux-Port*

Rue de la Commune at Boul. St-Laurent. 514-496-7678. www.quaysoftheoldport.com. Open Dec 6–Mar 7 Mon–Wed 11am–9pm, Thu–Fri 11am–10pm, weekends 10am–10pm. $3 per person (children under 6 free; family discounts available). Métro Place-d'Armes or Champ-de-Mars, orange line.

Skate safely right in Montreal harbour, even during the January thaw! Bonsecours Basin is an artificial ice surface with the river on three sides, chilled for 100 days a year. Once the St. Lawrence freezes several feet down, you can head farther out, under the watchful eye of attendants. Skate rentals *($6)* and free lockers (bring your own lock) are available.

. . . and Skating In

L'Atrium Le 1000 de la Gauchetière

1000 Rue de la Gauchetière, 514-395-0555. www.le1000.com. Open Oct 12–Easter Sun–Thu 11:30am–9pm, Fri–Sat 11:30am–midnight. Rest of the year Sun & Tue–Fri 11:30am–6pm, Sat 11:30am–10pm. $5.75. Métro Bonaventure, orange line.

Skate any time of the year on *the* indoor rink, under an immense glass dome. This palace of skating sits on the ground floor of "Le Mille," one of Montreal's break-the-mold new office towers with a signature peaked roof. Never been on blades? No worries—lessons are available.

Swimming Indoors . . .

Olympic Pool   *Piscine Olympique*

4141 Ave. Pierre-De-Coubertin, in Olympic Park. 514-252-4622. www.rio.gouv.qc.ca. $4 adults, $3 children. Open year-round Mon–Fri 7:30am–3pm & 6:30–10pm, weekends 9am–4pm. Métro Pie-IX or Viau, green line.

La Piscine Olympique is the Colosseum of pools—cavernous, skylit, with diving towers and swimming options ranging from a wading pool to one that's twice the size of a skating rink—altogether a great splash in any season.

. . . and Out

Notre Dame Island Beach

Île Notre-Dame. Access via Pont de la Concorde (Concorde Bridge). 514-872-6120. www.parcjeandrapeau.com. Open Jun 20–Aug 19 10am–7pm. $7.50. Boats $14–$25/hour. Métro Jean-Drapeau, yellow line, & bus 167.

The best place for outdoor swimming (and sailing, windsurfing, kayaking and pedal-boating) is at the lake on **Notre Dame Island★**, which is cleansed by plants in the adjacent lagoon. Here, the beach is sandy and you can rent almost anything you need.

Ski In The City

Parc du Mont-Royal. Take Voie Camillien-Houde or Chemin Remembrance to the parking areas. Métro Mont-Royal, orange line, then bus 11. Parc Nature du Cap St-Jacques; 514-280-6871; Métro Côte-Vertu, then bus 64 then bus 68.

Bring your cross-country skis (or snowshoes, for that matter), or rent from a shop. The "country" is right in town.

Mount Royal Park★★
Parc du Mont-Royal

Swish through a silent wintry wood on the fresh snow, under branches shedding a white cascade. Traverse a gentle slope, slide across a near-deserted meadow, glide around a bend and behold the city below. This is cross-country skiing in Mount Royal Park, only minutes from most hotels.

Cape St. Jacques Nature Park   *Parc-nature cap-St-Jacques*

205 Chemin du Cap-St-Jacques at Boul. Gouin, Pierrefonds. 514-280-6871. http://services.ville.montreal.qc.ca/parcs-nature.

Head to the west of the island and through groves of maple and across creeks, with only squirrels and occasionally a fox to watch your passage. At 267ha/ 659 acres, Cape St. Jacques is the largest expanse of undisturbed rusticity in Montreal, with a historic stone château and farmhouse to boot.

Winter Carnival   *Fête des Neiges*

Jean Drapeau Park, Île Ste-Hélène. Access via Pont Jacques-Cartier (Jacques-Cartier Bridge). 514-872-6120. www.fetedesneiges.com. Open weekends late Jan–early Feb 10am– 5pm. Admission is free, fee for some activities. Métro Jean-Drapeau, yellow line, & bus 167.

It's all about oversized snowmen, tobogganing down giant slides; ogling giant ice sculptures and creating smaller ones yourself; and conquering the North with a sled and a dog team. Montreal's *Fête des Neiges* is winter from the good old days, done Quebec-style, with servings of hot *poutine* (french fries smothered with gravy and cheese) and maple sugar on snow. You can rent all the equipment you'll need on-site, so there's no excuse not to join the fun.

. . . and a Carnival All Winter

Winter Carnival runs over three weekends from late January into February. Montreal's boroughs (*arrondissements*) hold their own carnivals as well during the cold months.

Festival Fun

You can hear jazz in Montreal all year, but the city is a mecca for the greats in July during the annual **Jazz Festival**. Extraordinary movies are on-screen for the World Film festival. Then there are Just for Laughs and Nuits d'Afrique. Many a devotee leaves Montreal bug-eyed and satisfied after a full schedule of attendance; for the less fanatic, taking advantage of the festivities to see a performance or two is an absolute must. *For details about festivals, see Calendar of Events.*

Free Entertainment

Mix in with the crowds and join in the applause around a fire-eater, a team of jugglers, or a unicyclist on Rue Jeanne-Mance during the Jazz Fest. Roar at the edgy antics of an up-and-coming comedy duo on a lane off Rue St-Denis during the Just for Laughs Festival. Open your ears and your senses to the sweet sounds of a Dixieland band reverberating off the great indoor plaza of Complexe Desjardins. And when there's no formal festival, find an impromptu gathering around a street clown or a human statue (no charge, but small change is appreciated), on Place Jacques-Cartier and along Rue Saint-Paul in Old Montreal.

Festival Tents

Liquor and food laws—you can't even buy a hot dog from a street vendor in Montreal; it's prohibited by law—are relaxed during the Jazz Fest, the High Lights Festival, and whenever people gather for a recognized street event and are in need of refreshment. Pick up a paper cup of good Canadian beer from the sponsoring brewery, and, while you're at it, banter with the locals who have come downtown for the event, along with visitors from all over.

Where East Is North and Local Is Not Local

In Montreal, English usage (and French, for that matter) is strictly local, which is not necessarily *local* (the word for a telephone extension in Montreal).

"East" and "west" are never to be taken literally (or *est* and *ouest*, for that matter). East refers to the downriver flow of the St. Lawrence River. So, depending where you are as the river wraps around Montreal, "east" can be southeast, true east, nearly north, or, most often, northeast. Likewise, "north" means away from the St. Lawrence, which is actually toward the northwest. That means the sun can rise in the south, sort of.

Montreal has museums for kids, festivals for kids, and an amusement park almost in the middle of town. *C'est le fun!* Responsible youngsters just might wonder whether there's enough for their parents to do.

Montreal Insectarium★   *Insectarium de Montréal*

4581 Rue Sherbrooke Est, on the grounds of the Botanical Garden. 514-872-1400. www2.ville.montreal.qc.ca/insectarium. Open daily in summer, 9am–6pm; mid-Sept–Oct Tue–Sun 9am–9pm; rest of the year Tue–Sun 9am–5pm. $9.75 winter, $12.75 summer (includes Botanical Garden). Métro Pie-IX, green line, or bus 185; or take the free shuttle from Viau Métro.

Yummy! Ants for dinner! Those nice people at the Insectarium searched all over and came up with the perfect recipe—nachos 'n ants. Doesn't that make your mouth water? They can also fix farm-raised grasshoppers *au gratin*, or cricket maki. Gram for gram, insects have three times the protein of red meat, and are no shirkers in the calcium department, either. If you don't eat them, somebody or something else certainly will.

The folks at the Insectarium are just full of tidbits of arthropod information, as well as tasty tidbits. But they're more than just talk and snacks. They'll lead you through a cloud of monarch butterflies flapping softly against your skin, and on to sturdy, state-of-the-art greenhouses where insects from around the globe fly and hop about. In summer, you'll walk through gardens that are planted precisely to attract creepy-crawlies.

Homely, invisible or gorgeous, insects are part of our world, and the Insectarium gives them their rightful place, in the food chain, the environment, controlling pests, looking after the dirty work, and sometimes just being down-right pesky.

It's all wonderfully yucky, and in extremely good taste. (Bug spray is not required.)

Ice Skating at L'Atrium

1000 Rue de la Gauchetière. 514-395-0555. www.le1000.com. Open Oct 12–Easter Sun–Thu 11:30am–9pm, Fri & Sat 11:30am–midnight. Rest of the year Sun & Tue–Fri 11:30am–6pm, Sat 11:30am–10pm. $5.75. Métro Bonaventure, orange line.

It's what Montreal kids do, and what kids from anywhere do in Montreal: get out on the ice and skate. Kids skate all year under the dome at L'Atrium. No skates? Rent a pair. No experience? Take a lesson.

Montreal Science Centre (iSci)★
Centre des sciences de Montréal

King-Edward Pier, Old Port (Boul. St-Laurent at Rue de la Commune). 514-496-4724. www.montrealsciencecentre.com. Open late Apr–mid-Jun daily 10am–5pm; mid-Jun– early Sept Sun–Thu 10am–5pm & Fri–Sat 10am–9pm. Rest of the year Mon–Fri 9am– 4pm & Sat–Sun 10am-5pm. $10–$25 depending on facilities visited; discounts available for children and families. Métro Place d'Armes, orange line.

The "i" in iSci stands for "interactive," and this see-through steel-and-glass greenhouse is all about taking control of the science experience through computers and wizardry.

Dynamo's Lair – Kids up to seven enter the castle of Dynamo, the gentle dragon, to learn about science through interactive games.

IMAX films take you right into the action on a curving, oversized screen. Enjoy such movies as *Deep Sea* as a sensational experience or for their scientific content, or, preferably, both. Travelogues and seasonal specials (*Santa vs the Snowman*) are regular features. English and French soundtracks alternate.

Eureka! Hall – Explore health, your everyday environment, and strange-but-true physical forces through games and multimedia challenges.

Technocity Hall – Computers and robots, design, communication and energy are the featured zones. Immerse yourself in theory and practical applications.

La Ronde★

Jean Drapeau Park, Île Ste-Hélène. 514-397-2000. www.laronde.com. Open mid-late May weekends 10am-8pm, late May–mid-Jun 10am–8pm, mid-Jun–Aug 10am-10:30pm; Sept– Oct weekends & holidays noon-7 or 8 pm (from 10am Labour Day weekend). $36.04 adults, $23.09 under 54 inches. Parking: $13. Métro Jean Drapeau, then bus 167.

You don't have to drive for hours to get to *this* amusement park. La Ronde enjoys a prime location on Île Ste-Hélène in the St. Lawrence River, opposite downtown. Give your teens Métro tickets and admission money, and let them loose on Vertigo, Vampire, Le Monstre, Cobra, Boomerang, L'Orbite, or Manitou, the aboriginal-inspired ride—or is it revenge?

Attractions have been climbing higher and spinning faster since Six Flags took over the park, and La Ronde has gone from a charming city-owned backwater to the big leagues of summer fun.

If thrill rides aren't your thing, try the tamer log-flume and bumper cars. The truly motion-shy can opt for concerts, magicians and street entertainers, at a reduced admission rate. And there's no better vantage point for the World Fireworks Competition in summer than La Ronde.

Festival Fun for Kids

Who said the Jazz Fest was only for grown-ups? They set up great big inflatable slides and games in Place des Arts every afternoon during the festival. Clowns are out painting faces. And there go the acrobats piling atop each other on Rue Jeanne-Mance, and a unicyclist riding backwards while he juggles. And did you see the fire-eater? It only costs the spare change that mom and dad care to contribute to the performers. And hey, the music's not bad, either.

During the Just for Laughs Festival, all those vaudeville acts and jokesters perform on the streets in the Latin Quarter. They speak three languages—English, French and/or pantomime—and, of course, kids are better at getting the joke than anyone else, even if they don't understand every word.

Street Fun

Even if there's no festival during your visit, there's always plenty of street fun in Montreal. Head to Place Jacques-Cartier in Old Montreal, or right down to the Old Port, where face-painters, balloon-twisting artists, sword-swallowers and performers of a dozen arts and entertainments vie for your attention, your hearts, and your spare change.

Festivals Just for Kids

Montreal has plenty for kids at its festivals, and also festivals that are just for kids.

La Fête des enfants *(Children's Festival)* draws 100,000 participants in August to rides, Native dances, concerts of Quebec music, and, yes, insect tastings. It's held at Maisonneuve Park, the Biodôme, and the Insectarium (all near the Olympic stadium), and most of the events are free. *For details: 514-872-0060 or www.ville.montreal.qc.ca/fetedesenfants.*

Montreal's World Film Festival is so big that it has an offspring, the **International Children's Film Festival**, held in March *(514-842-7750; www.fifem.com)*. At other times of the year, unusual films for children from around the world are shown in the cine-Kids program at **ex-Centris** on weekends *(3536 Boul. St-Laurent; 514-847-2206; www.ex-centris.com; see Performing Arts).*

Winter Carnival *(Fête des Neiges)* is open to adults, too, but grown-ups are often pushed aside by kids racing to the toboggan and tube slides. *See Musts for Fun.*

Excursions for Fun

The Cosmodôme★★

2150 Laurentian Autoroute, Laval. 12km/7mi northwest of Montreal via Hwy. 15 to Exit Boul. St-Martin. 450-978-3600. www.cosmodome.org. Open year-round Tue–Sun 10am–5pm; also Mon late Jun–Labour Day & holiday Mondays. Métro Henri-Bourassa, orange line, then bus 60 or 61. $11.50 adults, $7.50 children (self-guided visit).

Take the grand tour of the solar system throughout its turbulent history, and from earth to the limits of imagination. Learn how space and space science work magic on farming, mining, communications, and eavesdropping. Videos, sound effects and computer-controlled lighting make the show almost as impressive as space exploration itself.

Space Training – The Cosmodôme's **Space Camp Canada** is a hands-on experience for prospective astronauts, using a duplicate of the Endeavour shuttle, simulators, an anti-gravity chair, and motorized mobility units. Climb onto the Multi-Axis Trainer for a taste of twisting, twirling disorientation—it's the La Ronde of the stratosphere. Multi-day training sessions may be scheduled.

Canadian Railway Museum★   *Exporail*

110 Rue St-Pierre, St-Constant. 20km/12mi south of Montreal. Take Autoroute 15 South to Hwy. 132 West, then go south on Hwy. 209. 450-632-2410. www.exporail.org. Open May 15–early Sept 10am–6pm; early Sept–Oct Wed–Sun 10am–5pm; Nov–Apr weekends 10am–5pm. $12 adults, $7 children (ages 13-17), $6 children under 13.

Steam locomotives and passenger cars of times gone by are on display at the Canadian Railway Museum, and some of them are even living productive second lives. Forty-five of the greatest oldies are lovingly cared for and sheltered indoors. Treasures include the opulent private car of Canadian Pacific Railway magnate William Van Horne; the oldest steam locomotive built in Canada; and Montreal's first electric streetcar, the Rocket.

All Aboard!

At Exporail, the real fun takes place on Sundays. Attendants spend hours building up a head of steam on a vintage locomotive. When it's ready to go, you can climb on, and travel a kilometre or two through the countryside, then back to the museum.

With a landmark arts complex, a former vaudeville house, and the old Stock Exchange, Montreal has some first-rate performance venues to offer—not to mention the shows themselves.

Place des Arts★★

175 Rue Ste-Catherine Ouest. 514-842-2112. www.pdarts.com. Open daily and for performances. Métro Place des Arts, green line. See Landmarks.

That's "Plaza of the Arts," and no name is more accurate. Montreal's premier locale for live entertainment consists of three structures bordering a central square: a concert hall, a theatre building and the **Montreal Contemporary Art Museum★★** *(see Museums)*. The plaza hosts everything from full-scale opera to touring Broadway musicals, ballet, film festivals, and a full schedule of seasonal outdoor events.

Venues and Virtuosos

Salle Wilfrid-Pelletier is home to the Orchestre Symphonique (Montreal Symphony Orchestra, or MSO), the Opéra de Montréal, and Les Grands Ballets, as well as host to major touring shows. **Théâtre Jean-Duceppe** has its own company. **Théâtre Maisonneuve** is a large multipurpose hall. Also here are the smaller **Studio Théâtre** and **Théâtre Café de la Place**.

Tickets, not TKTS

Where to book your tickets for entertainment in Montreal? You probably don't want to spend your valuable travel time running from window to window (and hoping that they're open). Fortunately, you can make arrangements by phone or through the Web. Currently, there's no formal marketplace for last-minute unsold tickets, so book early.

- For **Place des Arts**, go to www.pdarts.com and and click "Show" and then the "Tickets" link; call 514-842-2112 or 866-842-2112; or visit the box office *(entrance off Rue Ste-Catherine; open Mon–Sat 10an–9pm)*.
- For many other venues and shows, you can purchase tickets at www.ticketpro.ca *(514-908-9090 or 866-908-9090)* or www.admission.com *(514-790-1245 or 800-361-4595)*. Many venues such as the Spectrum *(see Nightlife)*, as well as festivals such as the Jazz Fest and FrancoFolies *(see Calendar of Events and p 77)* sell tickets through these facilities.

Companies That Play the Place

- **L'Opéra de Montréal** – *514-985-2258. www.operademontreal.com.*
- **Orchestre Symphonique de Montréal** – *514-842-9951. www.osm.ca.*
- **Compagnie Jean-Duceppe** – *514-842-2212. www.duceppe.com.* Live theatre in French.
- **Orchestre Métropolitain du Grand Montréal** – *514-598-0870. www.orchestremetropolitain.com.* Montreal's *other* main orchestra performs in Place des Arts, St. John the Baptist Church, and free of charge in the summer at Théâtre de Verdure in La Fontaine Park *(see Parks and Gardens).*

Bell Centre

1260 Rue de la Gauchetière Ouest. 514-989-2841. www.centrebell.ca. Métro Bonaventure, orange line.

When Montreal's hockey palace isn't hosting the legendary *Canadiens*, it stages rock concerts featuring stars too mega to be contained in Place des Arts. Occasionally, even the Bell Centre will prove insufficient, and a show will book the **Olympic Stadium** in **Olympic Park★★**.

Centaur Theatre

453 Rue St-François-Xavier. 514-288-3161. www.centaurtheatre.com. Métro Place-d'Armes, orange line.

Montreal's main English-language theatre operates in modern, relatively intimate halls built into the former quarters of the Stock Exchange.

Centre Pierre-Péladeau

300 Boul. de Maisonneuve Est. 514-987-4691. www.centrepierrepeladeau.com. Métro Berri-UQAM.

Montreal's newest major performance centre, endowed by (and named for) a newspaper magnate, operates in cooperation with the Université du Québec à Montréal. It includes ultra-sleek, state-of-the-art Salle Pierre-Mercure. Jazz, classical music, dance, world music, and lectures are on the program, and some Saturday-afternoon events are free.

Saidye Bronfman Centre for the Arts

5170 Chemin de la Côte-Ste-Catherine. 514-739-2301. www.saidyebronfman.org. Métro Côte Ste-Catherine, orange line.

Montreal's Jewish museum and cultural centre features unusual productions, from Yiddish adaptations of French-Canadian works, to classics in English and French.

Théâtrical Café-Sitting

If you miss the performance at Théâtre du Nouveau Monde, there's always another show of intellectual debate and animated discussion in its **Café du Nouveau Monde**. Keep your eyes and ears open in the upstairs restaurant, or the café-bar that overflows to the sidewalk in warmer weather. The fare is French and bistro European, and you can order anything from a beverage only to fresh tuna carpaccio to merguez couscous.

Théâtre du Nouveau Monde

84 Rue Ste-Catherine Ouest. 514-866-8668. www.tnm.qc.ca. Métro Place-des-Arts.

The "New World Theatre" opened in 1912 as the Gayety vaudeville house, changed into a striptease joint (Lili St-Cyr was a featured artist), and served as a cinema. Now it's been lovingly restored, and regularly features French-language classics and avant-garde works, as well as Shakespeare and contemporary playwrights adapted into French.

Théâtre St-Denis [T]

[T] refers to map p36. 1594 Rue St-Denis. 514-849-4211. www.theatrestdenis.com. Métro Berri-UQAM.

In the heart of the Latin Quarter, Théâtre St-Denis is *the* place to see French-language music-hall shows, popular singers and comedy.

Théâtre de Verdure

In La Fontaine Park, Rue Sherbrooke at Ave. Parc-La Fontaine. 514-873-2015.
Métro Sherbrooke, orange line.

Montreal's best outdoor summer performance venue fits into a natural bowl, with plenty of overflow seating on the hillside above. Classical music, Shakespeare, and dance recitals by the city's major companies are all presented at no charge on summer nights. Seating is on metal benches.

Cinema Out of the Ordinary

ex-Centris – *3536 Boul. St-Laurent. 514-847-2206. www.ex-centris.com. Open from noon. $7.50 to $10. Métro St-Laurent, green line.*

At ex-Centris, you'll experience the movies as you've never experienced them. Software mogul Daniel Langlois took his millions and invested them where his heart was, to build a cinema and a new media complex into and around pre-existing neighbourhood commercial structures. Even if you're not in town for a movie, stop by ex-Centris for a look at the movie-going experience as it *could* be.

• **Out of the Ordinary 1** – Movies invite you to suspend disbelief. At ex-Centris, the experience starts at the ticket booth. In place of a counter with popcorn and soft drinks, there's a stylish, subtly lit bistro with fine food on two levels. And the three screening halls are fitted with plush seats and generous legroom.

• **Out of the Ordinary 2** – Many of the movies shown at ex-Centris won't be seen elsewhere in Canada or in the States, outside of film festivals. Experimental, daring, in exotic languages, challenging . . . whatever keeps a movie out of the local multiplex could earn it a place on ex-Centris' program. Some sound tracks are in English; subtitles are usually in French.

Festivals of the Arts

In Montreal the whole city's a stage for classical music and jazz, live theatre, and more. Time your visit to coincide with the arts festival that pleases your senses, or check the **Calendar of Events** at the beginning of this guide to find out what's happening when you're in town. Here's a taste of festival fare:

February

Port Symphonies – Ships' horns and locomotive whistles toot and the bells of Notre Dame Cathedral peal out music at the Old Port as it's rarely heard anywhere.

May

Festival TransAmériques – The best and the most promising contemporary theatre and dance companies from all over the hemisphere gather and perform in Montreal.

Chamber Music Festival – Performances are given at the chalet in Mount Royal Park, in the streets of Old Montreal, and at the Bon-Pasteur Chapel.

June

Fringe Festival – If it's daring and if it's theatre or dance or music, it's in the Fringe Festival in the Plateau Mont-Royal district.

July

Festival International de Jazz de Montréal – The greatest names in jazz and its offshoots, and some who will be great, assemble in Montreal for both paid and free performances.

Festival International de Lanaudière – The must-see summer festival for classical music takes place in the beautiful countryside northeast of Montreal.

Nuits d'Afrique – Sultry rhythms and tropical beats take over the streets and stages, day and night, in this annual food festival.

August

Les FrancoFolies – The melodies and lyrics of French composers will make you laugh or move you to tears, even if you don't understand a word.

October

Festival International de Nouvelle Danse – The borders between dance, ballet and acrobatics disappear in the annual celebration of new dance.

Orgue et couleurs – The organ is the centrepiece in concerts of classical and contemporary music.

November

Coup de Coeur Francophone – Celebrate the art of the *chanson*, the best in French lyrics.

Start with a Canadian dollar that can drop against its US counterpart. Add Quebec fashion flair, and a range of quality local products from maple syrup to soapstone carvings. Stir in extraordinary know-how in the design of retail emporia, and you've got a recipe for shopping, shopping, and more shopping.

Stores are generally open Mon–Wed 9am–6 or 7pm, Thu–Fri 9am–9pm, Sat 10am–5pm, and Sun noon–5pm, with extended hours before Christmas.

Bonsecours Market★   *Marché Bonsecours*

350 Rue St-Paul Est. 514-872-7730. www.marchebonsecours.qc.ca. Open summer daily, 10am-9pm; Apr-summer Sat-Wed 10am-6pm, Thu & Fri 10am-9pm; Labor Day-Oct Sun-Wed 10am-6pm, Thu-Sat 10am-9pm; Jan-Mar 10am-6pm.. Métro Champ-de-Mars, orange line. See Historic Sites.

The old market in Old Montreal is not just a historic site, it's a gathering of some of the leaders in design. The **Galerie des métiers d'art** is a fine crafts exhibition centre, as well as a shop. Items available elsewhere in the building include Inuit soapstone carvings and Native Canadian crafts; blown glass (with on-site demonstrations) at **Studio gogo glass**; and *prêt-à-porter* (ready-to-wear) fashions.

Gourmet Gifts

Maple syrup and smoked salmon are mainstays at hotel gift shops, but you'll find a more varied assortment of gourmet products at **Chez l'Epicier**, across from Bonsecours Market *(311 Rue St-Paul Est; 514-878-2232; www.chezlepicier.com)*. House specialties include award-winning maple syrup flavoured with rum or blueberries, and smoked lamb, duck and bison.

Rue Crescent★

Around the intersection of Rue Crescent with Rue Sainte-Catherine you'll find the "labels," from home-grown Parasuco to Mexx, Guess, Bennetton, and Canadian icon Roots. The exchange rate may make the wares along Rue Crescent a good bargain for American shoppers, even if the stores aren't having a sale.

Rue Saint-Denis★

From Rue Sherbrooke to Rue Duluth.

If there's a new twist to anything, you'll find it on Rue Saint-Denis in the trendy Plateau Mont-Royal section just north of Rue Sherbrooke and the Latin Quarter. One of the most "in" streets for seeing and being seen is also

the home of leading-edge clothing, jewellery, and, yes, bread and soap designers. Of course, trendy retailers like Gap and Mexx have moved in, as well. A Quebec icon of cold-weather clothing is **Kanuk**, off Saint-Denis at 485 Rue Rachel Est.

Downtown Department and Fashion Stores

Les Ailes de la Mode – *677 Ste-Catherine Ouest. 514-282-4537. www.lesailes.com.* Part of the former Eaton's department store is now a high-end emporium of eye-catching fashion. Some of the cherished Art Deco features of the former occupant remain.

La Baie – *Rue Ste-Catherine at Ave. Union. 514-281-4422. www.hbc.com.* A Canadian institution, this downtown department store lives on in Montreal as La Baie (short for *Compagnie de la Baie d'Hudson*, or Hudson's Bay Company). Hudson's Bay blankets are for many the emblem of the North. Look inside for gifts, delicacies, and everything else with a Canadian slant.

Birks – *1240 Phillips Square, opposite La Baie. 514-297-2511. www.birks.com.* This long-established jewellery and furnishings store occupies a place comparable to Tiffany's in New York, but it's more affordable. Check out the window displays, at the very least.

Ogilvy's – *1307 Ste-Catherine Ouest. 514-842-7711.* It used to be a legendary department store where the bagpipes played in the afternoon. Now it's a collection of boutiques that maintain heritage fixtures and many traditions, including the Christmas window display.

Simons – *977 Ste-Catherine Ouest. 514-282-1840.* High quality, down-to-earth prices, and styling with flair are characteristics of this Quebec City-based store, which took Montreal (and the former Simpson's department store) by storm a few years ago.

Underground City

Place Montreal-Trust, Eaton Centre, Promenades de la Cathédrale, Place Ville-Marie. See map pp 32–33.

On a day that's too cold or too hot for the outdoors, or simply because there are so many must-buys in Montreal, head to one of the shopping complexes that connect via the Underground City. Unlike some of the other retailers, Eaton Centre is open until 9pm *(Mon–Fri)*.

Public Markets

For the fun of shopping alongside locals, head for Montreal's public markets. Outdoor stands overflow with produce during mild weather, and the indoor shops of Montreal's markets remain busy every day of the year. *www.marchepublics-mtl.com.*

Atwater Market *(see Musts for Fun)* has ingredients for French cuisine, exotic coffees, and hand-made chocolates, as well as Latin American and West Indian food.

Jean Talon Market *(Métro Jean Talon, Orange Line)*, in Montreal's Little Italy, features cured and packaged delicacies that reflect English, French, Italian and Native American traditions: maple products (including maple ice wine), venison, buffalo, and Brome Lake duck. What you can't take home with you can be consumed on the spot.

Mega Malls

Canada embraced, refined, and perfected the indoor suburban shopping mall, and several vast examples lie within easy Métro reach of downtown Montreal.

Carrefour Angrignon

7077 Boul. Newman, La Salle. www.carrefourangrignon.com. Métro Angrignon, green line.

Located in the southwestern La Salle neighbourhood, Carrefour Angrignon serves a mixed English- and French-speaking area, with stores ranging from Sears to Gap to Canadian Tire (a hardware icon) and a discount supermarket.

Place Versailles

7275 Rue Sherbrooke Est. 514-353-5940. www.placeversailles.com. Métro Radisson, orange line.

The largest mall in the region has 225 stores, ranging from a branch of department store La Baie to Quebec-only labels to Bikili Village to a one-of-a-kind coin dealer and the ever-present lottery counter. The location is perfect for a shopping outing after a ball game at Olympic Stadium or a visit to the **Insectarium★** *(see Musts for Kids)* and **Botanical Garden★★** *(see Parks and Gardens).*

Museum Shops

Yes, there are T-shirts in museum boutiques, but also one-of-a-kind items you won't find elsewhere. And no museum admission is required.

Montreal Contemporary Art Museum★★

185 Rue Ste-Catherine Ouest. See Museums.

The shop here is accessible, not highbrow, in keeping with the museum's mission of modern-art outreach. Jewellery by local artists is featured.

Montreal Museum of Archaeology and History★★

350 Place Royale at Rue de la Commune. See Museums.

You'll find an excellent selection of wood and metal crafts, blown glass and fine jewellery.

Montreal Museum of Fine Arts★★

1380 Rue Sherbrooke Ouest. See Museums.

The museum shop features catalogs of current exhibitions and prints, and limited-edition household wares and fine crafts from far corners of the world.

Something Old

Rue Notre-Dame, from Rue Atwater to Ruy Guy; and Rue Amherst north of Rue Ste-Catherine. Montreal just oozes old furniture, furnishings and fittings at prices that attract antique dealers from New England and farther away. Browse the shops along Rue Notre Dame for pine tables, classic bathroom fittings, and stained-glass windows dating back to the 19C. Furniture of the French regime is hard to find, but excellent reproductions are available on Rue St-Paul in Old Montreal, and in Bonsecours Market.

Neighbourhoods for Shopping

The Fur District

Politically incorrect though it may be, the commerce that built Montreal lives on. Most fur garments in Canada are crafted by hand in a few commercial buildings around Rue Bleury and Rue Mayor in the eastern part of downtown. If you're lucky, you might even see pelts being sorted and graded.

Here's a sampling of showrooms:

Alexandor Furs – *2055 Rue Peel. 514-288-1119. www.alexandorfurs.com.*
Grossman Furs – *9250 Ave. du Parc. 514-288-3239.*
Hercules Furs – *350 Rue Mayor. 514-842-2492. http://pages.infinit.net/herc.*
McComber – *402 Boul. de Maisonneuve Ouest. 514-845-1167.*
Mega Furs– *397 Rue Mayor. 514-844-8651.*
North Pole Furs – *366 Rue Mayor. 514-842-7969. www.northpolefurs.com.*

Gallery Row

Rue Sherbrooke Ouest of Rue Crescent.

The district around the Museum of Fine Arts is also prime territory for finding paintings by contemporary Quebec and Canadian artists. Browse the windows on both sides of Sherbrooke west of the museum.

Outremont

Sedate, classy, well-off . . . that's Outremont, the *crème de la crème* of French-speaking neighbourhoods in Montreal *(see Neighbourhoods)*. Pastry shops, boutiques, specialty cheese shops and bistros can easily absorb a full day of browsing.

Avenue Laurier – *West of Boul. St-Laurent, Métro Laurier, orange line.*

Along Outremont's main commercial thoroughfare, you can acquire body potions at the flagship boutique of Quebec's own **Lise Watier** *(no. 392; 514-270-9296; www.lisewatier.com).* **La Cache** *(no. 1051; 514-273-9700),* one of the original stores of the chain known elsewhere as April Cornell, carries fashions and furnishings. **Jet-Setter** *(no. 66; 514-271-5058)* is the only authorized outlet in Montreal for famed Tilley Endurables travel goods.

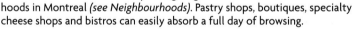

Must Not Take Home

One of the great attractions of Montreal shopping—for some Americans, at least—is that Cuban rum and cigars are freely available. US customs officials at Montreal airports and the border are ever on the watch for these items. But it's perfectly legal to puff away on an Uppmann cigar or imbibe Havana Club rum in Canada. Just make sure you dispose of the contents, bottles and wrappers before you leave the country.

Havana Club rum is available in any bar, or by the bottle in provincial liquor outlets (branded SAQ, or Societé des Alcools du Québec). Cuban cigars are less widely available, but are stocked by specialty tobacco shops, such as **Casa del Habano** *(1434 Rue Sherbrooke Ouest; 514-849-0037; www.lacasadelhabano.com).*

Montreal by night has always had its exotic, forbidden and edgy side, from flowing booze during American Prohibition to a tour by a girl band from Cuba today. And then there's traditional French-Canadian conviviality. Strangers and visitors join in singing and laughing as part of one big family. Add a choice of languages, and you have several cities' worth of entertainment.

Cabaret du Casino

Montreal Casino, Île Notre-Dame. Access via Pont de la Concorde (Concorde Bridge). 514-392-2746. www.casinos-quebec.com. Métro Jean-Drapeau, yellow line, & bus 167.

The stars might not be household names, but the production numbers are elaborate, much of the music is familiar, and you get it all for a song.

Café Campus

57 Rue Prince-Arthur Est, Plateau Mont-Royal. 514-844-1010. Métro Sherbrooke, orange line.

Its' no coincidence that Montreal's favourite nightclub with the 20-something set is located in the liveliest section of the Plateau Mont-Royal district. Pedestrians-only Rue Prince-Arthur is a show in itself at all hours year-round.

Club Balattou

4372 Boul. St-Laurent, Plateau Mont-Royal. 514-845-5447. www.nuitsdafrique.com. Métro Mont-Royal, orange line.

You can find the likes of Club Balattou in Paris or Marseilles: pulsing French rhythms from Africa North and Equatorial, a festival of music from the Maghreb, and artists who attend classes or drive taxis by day and perform by night for their own pleasure as well as yours.

Comedy Nest

2313 Rue Ste-Catherine Ouest at Atwater, Downtown. 514-932-6378. www.thecomedynest.com. Métro Atwater, green line.

Some comedy travels, some doesn't, but you're sure to find laughs among Montreal's English-language performers on the third floor of the entertainment complex in the Forum, Montreal's one-time palace of hockey.

Les Deux Pierrots

104 Rue St-Paul Est, Old Montreal. 514-861-1270. www.lespierrots.com. Winter open Fri–Sat only; rest of the year Wed–Sun from 8pm. Métro Place d'Armes, orange line.

A *boîte à chansons*—a song club—is Quebec's home-grown version of karaoke—joining in the singing is de rigueur. Don't think it's only foot-stomping French-Canadian folk music, either. There are western evenings and ska and punk rock and ballads, in English as well as French. The common denominator is continuing interaction between performers and spectators.

Le Festin du Gouverneur

Old Fort, Île Ste-Hélène. Access via Pont Jacques-Cartier (Jacques Cartier Bridge). 514-879-1141. www.festin.com. May–Oct daily 6:30pm. Rest of the year Wed–Sat 7pm. Métro Jean-Drapeau, yellow line.

You get dinner, dessert, and a musical trip into history at Festin du Gouvernor. Characters from New France return to life with clapping and foot-stomping and a bit of vaudeville that leaves no room for wallflowers.

House of Jazz

2060 Rue Aylmer, Downtown. 514-842-8656. Métro McGill, green line.

Jazz rules in Montreal, and not just during the summer Jazz Fest. Oscar Peterson was born and raised here, and Charles Biddle for years ran this establishment under his own name. The sweet music still plays nightly, and chicken and ribs are the favoured fare.

Hard Rock Cafe

1458 Rue Crescent. 514-987-1420. www.hardrock.com. Métro Guy-Concordia, green line.

Check into the Hard Rock when you're in Montreal for a familiar combination of rock and roll memorabilia, a huge dance floor, and Cajun and southwest dishes. And while you're at it, check out the Winston Churchill Pub, Newtown, and Les Beaux Jeudi, along English Montreal's late-night party block.

Le Spectrum

318, Rue Ste-Catherine Ouest, Downtown. 514-861-5851. Tickets: 514-908-9090 or 866-908-9090. www.metropolismontreal.ca/spectrum. Métro Place-des-Arts, green line.

This ex-movie house is Quebec's classic rock concert hall, with cabaret-style seating and presentation. Sting, Peter Gabriel and Tina Turner have all played the Spectrum, along with Quebec headliners Céline Dion, Abbittibbi, Leloup, and Marjo.

Le St-Sulpice

1680 Rue St-Denis, Latin Quarter. 514-844-9458. Métro Berri-UQAM.

Beer, dancing, and live music or a DJ are the attractions in every nook and cranny on three floors of this classic French-Canadian town house. The *terrasses* are staked out early in summer. Line-ups can be lengthy at this prime nightspot on the *rue*, but the host of clubs north on Rue St-Denis past Rue Sherbrooke, can absorb the overflow.

Upstairs Jazz Bar

1254 Rue McKay, Downtown. 514-931-6808. Métro Peel, green line.

Small quarters make the Upstairs—which is not upstairs—an intimate, easy-going lair, where musicians chat easily with patrons between sets, over steaks from the grill, quesadillas, and drinks from the bar.

Must Be Pampered: Spas

Ah, Montrealers. If their lives were ever stressful, you'd never know it from their sleek clothing, casual hairstyles perfectly in place, and radiance. It all comes naturally—with a little help from *le spa*.

AquaLüd Spa Concept

1484 Rue Sherbrooke West, third floor, Downtown. 514-938-3665. www.aqualudspa.com. Métro Guy-Concordia, green line.

AquaLüd offers a range of exotic and therapeutic scrubs, mud wraps and toning, manicures and pedicures, and, of course, massages—the house specialty is Thai-style. For an over-the-top experience, try AquaLüd's chocolate splash pedicure—a footbath in a yummy chocolate-raspberry fizz, followed by a chocolate-oil massage and hot wax coating. Beyond beauty, there are personal trainers on staff, as well as a stress-management specialist. Men are welcome with a specialized menu of facial and back treatments, scrubs and massages.

Atmosphère

475 Ave. President-Kennedy, in the Delta Montreal Hotel, Downtown. 514-286-1364. www.atmospherespa.qc.ca. Métro McGill, green line.

Atmosphère's location in the Delta Hotel enables the spa to complement its treatment offerings with the hotel's pool, sauna and whirlpool. Mainstays are massage treatments, balneotherapy, algae wraps and body peels. Packages range from a choice of one treatment paired with a 30-minute massage to a two-day menu of pampering with six treatments and snacks.

Rainspa

55 Rue Saint-Jacques Ouest, in the Hotel Place d'Armes, Old Montreal. 514-842-1887. Métro Place d'Armes, orange line.

Rainspa, on the third floor of the Hotel Place d'Armes, offers Swedish, hot stone, aromatherapy and shower massages along with body treatments. All packages include access to the hammam, Montreal's only Middle Eastern steam bath.

Spa Sinomonde

99 Ave. Viger Ouest, in the Holiday Inn Select, Old Montreal. 514-878-9888. Métro Place-d'Armes, orange line.

Spa Sinomonde offers fewer frills than other city spas, but the prices are quite reasonable—$63 for a one-hour Swedish or Shiatsu massage, or $15 for day use of the sauna, steam room, exercise room and whirlpool (otherwise included with the cost of a massage). And the location is convenient if you're staying in Old Montreal.

Tonic SalonSpa

3613 Boul. St-Laurent, Plateau Mont-Royal. 514-499-9494. www.tonicsalonspa.com. Métro Sherbrooke, orange line.

Expect something different, and a little laid-back in the trendy and offbeat Plateau Mont-Royal district north of downtown. You'll find table massages for $65 per hour, but also a warm-stone massage treatment, and chair massages available for as little as ten minutes—not to mention seductive Kama Sutra makeup, algae wraps, and the Himalayan combination (a sweat treatment, essential-oil inhalation, and five other treatments). Men feel more welcome here than at spas elsewhere in the city. A combination including a men's haircut, an hour-long massage and a facial costs about $145.

Destination: Spa Eastman

895 Chemin des Diligences, Eastman. 110km/69mi east of Montreal via Autoroute 10; take Exit 106 and follow signs in the village of Eastman. 450-297-3009 or 800-665-5272. www.spa-eastman.com.

Need a little more spa? Who doesn't? In about an hour, you can be well into the rolling countryside of the Eastern Townships, at a lakeside estate set amid forests, meadows and glades at the foot of Mount Orford.

The setting in itself will de-stress you from the moment you arrive, if not before; the treatments should further the effect, and create restorative memories. Drive out for the day, or stay overnight (there are 44 rooms). Facilities include an indoor and outdoor pool, a steam bath, a meditation room and exercise equipment. Spa Eastman specializes in rain massage (while being sprinkled by jets of warm water) and watsu (experience shiatsu massage in a pool of hot water), along with aesthetic services.

A half-day's stay, for $199 without overnight lodging, includes lunch, use of the pool and steam bath, and a choice of three treatments that can include massage, pressotherapy (a detoxifying treatment that stimulates lymph circulation in the legs by means of inflatable boots), and a body wrap followed by a hydromassage. The "getaway" program includes lunch and four treatments for $259.

• For those who can't get away, **Spa Eastman Montreal** offers many of the same services in a downtown setting *(666 Rue Sherbrooke Ouest, 16th floor; 514-845-8455; www.spaeastman.com; Métro McGill, green line).*

The walled capital of French-speaking North America makes a great day trip from Montreal (though you should stay longer!). And well within range—even by municipal bus in some cases—are historic villages, First Nations reserves, canals both old and new, mountains to ski and hike, and lakes set in the Canadian Shield.

Quebec City★★★

260km/161mi north of Montreal by Autoroute 20 or Autoroute 40.

Don't think of Quebec City as only a provincial capital. It's the spiritual home of one of Canada's two founding peoples, a fortress of national identity as well as a fortified city. Quebec City perches on a high point at a narrows— "kebec" in the Algonquian Amerindian language—where the St. Charles River flows into the St. Lawrence. Explorer Jacques Cartier landed here in 1535, and Samuel de Champlain set up a fur-trading post in 1608.

Today Nouvelle France is alive within the old city walls, fieldstone buildings with steeply pitched roofs, and narrow, winding streets. The battlefield of the Plains of Abraham recalls what's still known as *La Defaite* (The Defeat) by French Canadians. Indeed, Quebec City embodies a resolve to preserve, protect and develop the major French-speaking society in the Western Hemisphere.

Sophisticated Quebec City claims fine hotels, cutting-edge restaurants, a celebration of winter pleasures, and nearby ski resorts that make it a lively destination 365 days a year. Come in winter to experience the city shining against a carpet of snow, in spring or summer when flowers bloom alongside stone ramparts, or in fall when the countryside glows in shades of red and gold.

Lower Town★★★   *Basse-Ville*

Follow Rue du Petit-Champlain down from the ramparts of Quebec City to a 19C seaport. What began as a trading post was taken over by English merchants, who erected their banks, warehouses and docks along the waterside. The solid bones of those old buildings have in many cases been recycled into the charming hotels of today.

Place Royale★★

Bounded by Rue Notre-Dame & Rue St-Pierre between Rue Sous-le-Fort & Rue du Porche.

The main square of Lower Town, cobblestone Place Royale was the site of the settlement's early market.

On the north side of the square, you'll find a sculpture of Louis XIV of France; it's a copy of a marble sculpture made in 1665 by Bernini. Flanking the south side of the square, the **Church of Our Lady of Victories★** (*Église Notre-Dame-des-Victoires*) commemorates two early successes against the English. It was built between 1688 and 1723 as an auxilliary chapel to Quebec's main cathedral to serve the congregation in Lower Town.

Running along the east side of Place Royale, **Rue Saint-Pierre★** was the main business street of Quebec City in the 19C, home to the first insurance company in Canada, as well as banks and trading companies. Many of its buildings are wonderfully preserved. If you continue left on **Rue Saint-Paul★**, with its boutiques and restaurants housed in centuries-old brick buildings, you'll soon arrive at the **Old Port★** (*Vieux-Port*).

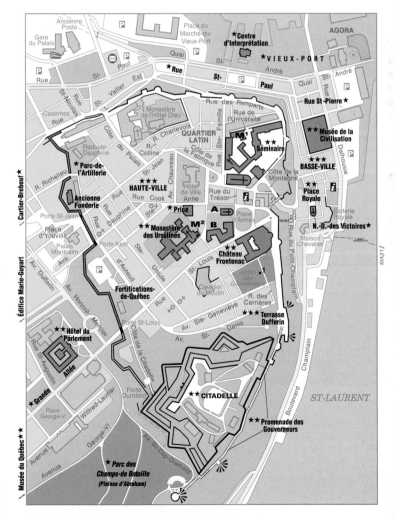

Museum of Civilization★★   *Musée de la civilisation*

85 Rue Dalhouse. 418-643-2158. www.mcq.org. $8. Open year-round Tue–Sun 10am–5pm.

Old Port Visitors' Centre★
Centre d'Interprétation du Vieux-Port-de-Québec

100 Quai St-André. 418-648-3300. www. pc.gc.ca/vieuxport. $4. Open daily early May–early Sept 10am–5pm, early Sept–early Oct noon–4pm. Time has passed since Quebec City was one of the major ports of the world, but the glory days are recalled here. A resident from the 18C guides you through the centre with tales of shipbuilding and timber harvesting up the St. Charles and St. Lawrence rivers. Walk upstairs to the terrace for superb views of Lower Town.

With all the civilization embodied in the buildings and culture of the Upper Town, a museum in the Lower Town had better be good. And it is.

The Museum of Civilization is architect Moshe Safdie's modern interpretation of Quebec's temples of old. Natural light floods down into exhibition spaces, while steep roof lines reflect those of the old city.

It's not quite an art museum, though it has paintings and sculptures. It's not a history or natural history museum, though it displays artifacts from cultures around the world, especially those of Quebec's Inuit and First Nations peoples. It's not an ethnology museum, though it exhibits costumes, and not a kids' museum, though there are always hands-on exhibitions. All together, it's a museum dedicated to being in touch with the human adventure here and everywhere, in the past, present and future.

Upper Town★★★   *Haute-Ville*

The narrow, winding streets, the massive stone walls, turrets and crenellations and gateways of Quebec City create a fairy-tale setting. It's all real, a living city where people come to work and shop, as well as relax and have fun and experience the *joie de vivre* of the Old Capital. It's Old Europe, with fieldstone buildings hugging each other close to the street. But it's also the new, with Quebec's signature steep roofs to shed the snow loads.

Wander at will in Quebec City's Upper Town. You won't run out of things to see, historical buildings to enchant you, lanes to follow, crannies to peek into, and cafes where you can sip an apéritif.

Place d'Armes★★

From the St. Louis Gate on the Grande Allée, head all the way down Rue St-Louis, to the main square of the old city. Once a parade and exercise ground for the troops of His Majesty the King of France, it became a public green space one hundred years ago. In the centre is the **Monument to Faith** (*Monument de la Foi*), a 1916 sculpture that recalls the arrival of the first priest to Quebec City in 1615.

Château Frontenac★★

1 Rue des Carrières. 418-692-3861. www.fairmont.ca. See Must Stay: Quebec City.

A hotel is a hotel, except when it's also a castle, and the most visible landmark of a city. Opened in 1893 by the Canadian Pacific Railway, the Château Frontenac takes its inspiration from the styles popular in Quebec City at the time, which in turn were inspired by the châteaux of France. Like a true castle, the Château Frontenac winds in several wings around a central courtyard, its brick and stone walls capped by steep copper roofs. In its day, the Château came to embody the brand image of the rail-way, and it was imitated to some degree—but never duplicated—in railway cities across Canada.

Try to spot the rooster claws on the façade above the coach gate—coat of arms of the Count of Frontenac, once the governor of New France. Inside the courtyard you'll find a stone relief of the Maltese Cross, taken from the residence of another governor.

Quebec Seminary★★   *Séminaire de Québec*

2 Côte de la Fabrique. 418-692-2843. www.seminairedequebec.org. Open Jun 23–Labour Day daily 9:30am–5:30pm. Rest of year Tue–Sun 10am–5pm. $5.

Quebec City's Laval University began right here in 1663 as a training school for priests. In the complex around a courtyard is the **Museum of French America [M¹]** (*Musée de l'Amérique Française; see map p 87*), housing historical documents, paintings, and precious religious articles. In the Demer building, you'll learn about the French-speaking communities of North America, in Quebec, Acadia, Louisiana, New England, and the Canadian West, which owe their origins to New France.

Ursuline Monastery★★   *Monastère des Ursulines*

12 Rue Donnacona. Chapel: 418-694-0413. Open May–Oct Tue–Sat 10am–11:30am & 1:30pm–4:30pm, Sun 1pm–5pm. Museum: 418-694-0694. $6. Open May–Sept Tue–Sat 10am–noon & 1pm–5pm, Sun 1pm–5pm; Oct–Nov and Feb–Apr Tue–Sun 1pm–5pm.

Talk about Old School—this is the oldest women's school in the hemisphere, and it's still going strong. Started in 1641, it has outlasted fires, conquest and renovations, all the while maintaining its extensive gardens and orchard. The **chapel** dates from early in the 20C, and has an inner sanctum restricted to use by nuns of the order.

The sculptures and other fine **ornamentation**★★ largely come from earlier constructions—many pieces were gilded by the sisters themselves. The **museum** in an adjacent house recalls the everyday life of the order through furnishings and documents.

Anglican Cathedral of the Holy Trinity★
La Cathédrale Holy Trinity

[A] *refers to map p 87. 31 Rue des Jardins. 418-692-2193. www.ogs.net/cathedral.*

Much maligned south of the border, King George III himself paid for the construction of the first Anglican cathedral outside the British Isles. If you've been to London, you'll recognise the similarity to St. Martin in the Fields. Alas, the model wasn't totally suitable, and the roof had to be raised to better shed snow in winter.

Old Courthouse★   *Ancien Palais de Justice*

[B] *refers to map p 87. 12 Rue St-Louis.*

This fine Second Empire edifice houses the provincial ministry of finance, but it's the layers of history that are worth noting. The coats of arms of explorers Jacques Cartier and Samuel de Champlain flank the entrance. The courthouse stands on the site of the original Recollet church.

Price Building★

65 Rue Sainte-Anne. Not everything in the Upper Town is as old as the Conquest. Quebec City's first skyscraper, dating from 1930, rose to all of 16 storeys in Art Deco style, with decorative elements—squirrels, pine cones—that made it unabashedly Canadian. Unusual for its day, the building's copper roof was a gesture to the architecture all around. Peek in at the bas-reliefs that decorate the entry.

The Fortifications of Quebec★★

The defenses of Quebec City weren't built only by the French. The British added Martello towers to the works of French military engineers, and completed the Citadel between 1820 and 1832. Once the British garrison moved on in 1871, Lord Dufferin, the governor general, decided on major renovations and restoration to beautify the city, and visitors are in his debt to this day.

The Citadel★★

South of the Upper Town, from inside the St-Louis Gate. 418-694-2815. www.lacitadelle. qc.ca. Visit by guided tour only, Apr 10am–4pm, May–Jun 9am–5pm, Jul–Aug 9am–6pm, Sept 9am–4pm, Oct 10am–3pm. Nov–Mar daily tour at 1:30pm. $8.

Sitting on the point of Cap Diamant—Quebec's Gibraltar—the Citadel stands watch over the river below, and the entry to the hinterland. Planned by the French, it was actually built starting in 1820 by the British, in a star-shaped layout. A system of fortified protuberances, or outworks, protected the landward side from attack, while cannon on solid ramparts guarded the city from a seaward assault. Had the French completed this wonderful defensive work earlier, they might have been spared the embarrassment of 1759, when the English approached unexpectedly from the landward side.

The Citadel is an active military base for the Royal 22nd Regiment—the French-speaking "Van-doos." Don't miss their **changing of the guard** ceremony, in full-dress scarlet uniform, at 10am from June 24 to the first weekend of September.

Governors' Walk★★   *Promenade des Gouverneurs*

Leave the Citadel by the Durnford Gate, take the path to the left and continue towards the St. Lawrence River.

Continue from the Citadel to **Dufferin Terrace★★★ *(Terrasse Dufferin)***, a wooden platform and public park conceived by Governor-General Dufferin to afford magnificent **views★★** of the river. Onward, just before the Château Frontenac in Jardin des Gouverneurs park, the **Wolfe-Montcalm Monument [1]** *(see map p 87)* commemorates the British and French commanders of 1759, who both died in battle.

Artillery Park National Historic Site★
Lieu historique national du Canada du Parc-de-l'Artillerie

2 Rue d'Auteuil. 418-648-4205. www.pc.gc.ca/artillery. Open daily Apr–Oct 10am–5pm. Nov–Mar by reservation. $4.

Continuing along the walls to face the modern city, you'll come to the site of a British artillery barracks, and later, a Canadian arms works and arsenal. The **Old Foundry** is the focal point for visits, and includes a scale model of Quebec City at the beginning of the 19C.

The New City★

From the St-Louis Gate, the **Grande Allée★** leads into the new city in appro-
priately grand fashion. Boutiques, restaurants and nightclubs line the allée's
sidewalks, and trees and 19C mansions and town houses give it the air of a
small-scale European boulevard.

Parliament Building★★   *Hôtel du Parlement*

*Visitor entrance at the corner of Grand Allée & Honoré-Mercier Ave. 418-643-7239. www.
assnat.qc.ca. Visit by guided tour only, Jun 24–Labour Day Mon–Fri 9am–4:30pm, weekends 10am–4:30pm. Rest of the year Mon–Fri 9am–4:30pm.*

Quebec's legislature, the National Assembly, sits in this
fine Second Empire building inaugurated in 1876. In
scale and size, it's reminiscent of city halls of the era in
other parts of the continent, but the decorative stonework and delicate ironwork give it a distinctively Parisian touch. Inside, the layout is based purely on British
parliamentary practice, with the government benches
facing those of the loyal opposition.

National Battlefields Park★   *Parc des Champs-de-Bataille*

*Plains of Abraham. 418-648-4071. www.ccbn-nbc.gc.ca. Discovery Pavilion open 24 Jun–
Labour Day 8:30am-5:30pm; rest of year Mon-Fri 8:30am–5pm, Sat 9am–5pm, Sun 10am–
5pm. $5.*

On September 13, 1759, British troops under General Wolfe scaled the unde-
fended cliffs below the Plains of Abraham, and in less than 15 minutes put an
end to the French Empire in North America. Skirmishes raged for several years,
but this is where the fate of the continent was decided. Three Martello towers
remain from the days of the British garrison, erected as a defense against the
Americans, who had occupied Quebec City during the winter of 1775-76.

On the grounds of the park is the **Quebec Museum of Fine Arts★★** *(Musée
national des beaux-arts du Québec)* housing significant Quebec art from the
last two centuries *(418-643-2150; www.mnba.qc.ca; open Jun–Labour Day daily
10am–6pm, rest of the year Tue–Sun 10am–5pm; Wed to 9pm all year; $12).*

Ice Hotel Quebec

*143 Rue Duchesnay, Pavillion l'Aigle, Ste-Catherine-de-la-Jacques-Cartier. 40km/25mi
northwest of Quebec City via Autoroute 40 west & Hwy. 367 north. 418-875-4522 or
877-505-0423. www.icehotel-canada.com. 32 rooms. Open Jan–Mar only.*

Remember to keep your nose outside the blankets, and that you don't really need ice
with that vodka cocktail. Wind chill doesn't apply when you're deep inside tons of ice
and snow, snug on a bed of animal hides. They're lining up to get into the Ice Hotel, so
you'll probably be allowed to stay only one night, weather permitting, of course. But
what a night! Packages include dinner at the adjacent Duchesnay resort.

The Eastern Townships★★
Cantons de l'Est or l'Estrie

Take Autoroute 10 (Autoroute des Cantons de l'Est), the Eastern Townships Autoroute directly east from Montreal.

The foothills of the Appalachians give the Townships their meadows and forests, punctuated by mountain ridges. Loyalists who fled the former American colonies after the Treaty of Separation gave the towns their character, as lost corners of New England. Descendents of the independent farmers and tradesmen who settled the Townships are now in the minority, but their old clapboard and brick farmhouses and red barns—quite different from the stone farmsteads of the St. Lawrence Valley—still dot the landscape. The Townships are a favourite area for skiing, hiking, antiquing, leaf-peeping in the fall, and just getting out into the fresh air of the country.

Granby Zoo★   *Jardin zoologique de Granby*

Granby, 83km/52mi east of Montreal via Autoroute 10 to Exit 68, north on Hwy. 139. 450-372-9113 or 877-472-6299. www.zoogranby.ca. Zoo & water park open late May–late June 10am–5pm, late June–Aug 10am–7pm; zoo open daily through Labour Day & weekends to early Oct 10am–5pm. $25 adults, $16 children under 12, children under 3 free.

Brilliant tropical parrots in the Great North? Why not! Not to mention Japanese monkeys, Siberian tigers, a snow leopard, and kangaroos and wallabees. This is an up-close zoo, and aquarium, too, where visitors can pass their hands through fur and feathers, pet nurse sharks and manta rays, and stare their animal friends straight in the eyes.

Lake Brome★   *Lac-Brome*

110km/68mi east of Montreal via Autoroute 10 east to Exit 90, then south on Hwy. 243.

Browse the antique shops, art galleries and boutiques in the community of Knowlton. Or, for an intense round of country fun, arrive for the **Brome Agricultural Fair** in early September. Lake Brome ducks are essential at any fine table in Quebec, and are always on the menu at local restaurants. Lake Brome, with its small public beach, is popular with windsurfers.

Brome County Historical Museum★ (*Musée historique du comté de Brome)*— *130 Rue Lakeside. 450-243-6782. Open mid-May–mid-Sept Mon–Sat 10am–4:30pm, Sun 11am–4:30pm. $5. www.townshipsheritage.com.* This collection of heritage buildings includes the original schoolhouse, fire house (converted to a general store), and brick courthouse.

Parc du Mont-Orford★

128km/80mi east of Montreal via Autoroute 10 east to Exit 115, then Hwy. 141 north. Skiing and golf: Chemin du Parc, 819-843-6548 or 866-673-6731; www.orford.com. Park: 819-843-9855; www.sepaq.com. General park use $3.50 daily, $5 parking, $8.78 additional for cross-country skiing.

An island of wilderness in a long-settled rural area, Mount Orford (850m/2,788ft) is best known for its family-oriented **downhill skiing**, with a vertical drop of 540m/1,771ft, and 54 trails. Every sort of skiing is available, from daredevil to beginner, and every sort of lift, from gondola to quadruple chairs to old-fashioned T-bar and rope tow. Cross-country ski and snowshoe trails wind through the lower part of the park. Come out in autumn to see the colours, and in summer for swimming, golfing, cycling and climbing, and to see concerts at the **Centre d'Arts Orford** *(Orford Arts Centre; 800-567-6155; www. arts-orford.org).*

St-Benoît-du-Lac Abbey★   *Abbaye de St-Benoît-du-Lac*

20km/12mi west of Magog via Route 112; turn south after 5km/3mi and continue 2km/1.24mi past Austin. 819-843-4080. www.st-benoit-du-lac.com. Open daily 9am–11am & for 11am & 5pm Mass except Thu.

The Benedictine abbey and its bell tower rise from a lakeside knoll as if they've always been there. Actually, the abbey was founded in 1924; most of the buildings went up in the 1930s according to the plans of re-nowned monk-architect Dom Paul Bellot, who is buried here. The church was consecrated in 1994.

The monks live lives of prayer and contemplation, but also of manual work. They run cheese and cider factories and an orchard, and accept both men and women for retreats *(reserve by telephone only).* Day visitors are welcome to browse the small shop and buy cheese until 10:45am, to hear 11am Mass, complete with Gregorian chants, and to hear vespers at 5pm (except on Thursday). At other times, you can appreciate the abbey from the waters of Lake Memphrémagog, and purchase the abbey's excellent L'Ermite and Mont-Saint-Benoît cheeses in shops nearby.

Sutton★

123km/77mi east of Montreal via Autoroute 10 to Exit 68, then south on Hwy. 139.

Settled by Americans in 1795, the village of Sutton claims an **Anglican Church** erected in 1850. Numerous boutiques and galleries are open all year; golfing is popular in summer.

Mount Sutton — *671 Maple Rd. 450-538-2545 or 866-538-2545. www.mt-sutton.com.*

One of the premier ski areas in the Townships, Mount Sutton offers 53 trails descending from a long ridge, including significant expanses of Quebec's famous glade skiing, a 968m/3,194ft summit, nine chairlifts, and a 455m/1,500ft vertical drop.

Lake Memphrémagog

124km/78mi east of Montreal via Autoroute 10 east to Exit 115 for Magog.

When you're on Memphrémagog, you're in international waters. The lake stretches 50km/31mi between ridges of mountains and hills from Magog down to Newport, Vermont. In decades past, lake steamers connected with stage coaches to provide transport to the south. Old inns along the way survive to cater to today's travellers, whether they're in search of traditional surroundings, or looking for Memphry *(Memphré)*, the monster who reputedly lurks beneath the waves. Winds are reliable, making Memphrémagog the preferred lake in Quebec for sailing and windsurfing.

Almost as pleasing as sailing or motorboating is exploring the winding roads above the lake by car, on foot or bicycle, catching the views to the Green Mountains of Vermont, and Mount Orford and Owl's Head nearby. The town of **Magog★** *(take Autoroute 10 to Hwy. 112)*, at the northern end of the lake, is a traditional summer resort centre with a theatre and marina.

Lake Cruises★

Cruises depart from Magog pier. 819-843-8068. www.croisiere-memphremagog.com. $20 (short cruise), $75 (day cruise) or $55 (dinner cruise). Operates mid-May–Jun 1 & Sept 4–Oct weekends 2pm; Jun–Sept 4, daily 9am–6pm. Call to reserve.

The best way to reach the hidden coves of Lake Memphrémagog and view its historic houses, lakeside estates, and the mountains to the west and south, is to board one of the cruise boats that make daily trips in summer. The 9am departure takes passengers all the way down to Newport, Vermont, and includes a one-hour stopover and lunch on board; it returns by 4pm. Shorter cruises of just under two hours head south to within view of the Abbey of St-Benoit-du-Lac.

The Laurentians★★   *Les Laurentides*

60km/37mi northwest of Montreal via Autoroute 15.

Some of the oldest mountains in the world . . . un-broken expanses of forest and crystal clear lakes by the hundreds . . . superb skiing and hiking and water sports and fishing . . . year-round resorts. All this starts within an hour's drive of Montreal.

Getting people to settle up here and farm the thin soil was a hard sell more than a century ago. With improved transportation, Montrealers began coming in droves to spend weekends in the fresh air and beautiful surroundings, and they haven't stopped since.

Peak viewing season for fall colours is generally mid-October, with variation from year to year. Most ski resorts have snowmaking equipment, and are in full operation before Christmas, and often into April.

Mont-Tremblant Park★   *Parc du Mont-Tremblant*

136km/84mi northwest of Montreal via Autoroute 15 & Hwy. 117 to St-Faustin, then north on Hwy. 1. Chemin du Lac-Supérieur, Lac-Supérieur. 819-688-2281 or 800 665-6527. www. sepaq.com. Day pass $3.50.

Tremblant the mountain only marks the beginning of a reserve of forests and lakes stretching over hundreds of square kilometres to the northeast. Deer, moose, black bears and wolves call the park home, along with the endangered bald eagle.

In winter, visitors may drive from Tremblant village and follow a road that winds along the twisting Rivière du Diable (Devil's River) to the Croches Falls, usually fully frozen in mid-plunge. Summer allows a circular trip along the river past the **Devil's Falls★** and **Muskrat Falls★**, and back to the southeast to continue to St-Donat and back toward Sainte-Agathe. Park adventures include cross-country skiing and snowshoeing in winter, and hiking, climbing, para-sailing, biking and fishing in summer. You can rent canoes and kayaks at Lac (Lake) Supérieur, east of Mont-Tremblant village.

Mont-Tremblant: Mountain, Village, Resort

At 875m/2,888ft, Tremblant is the tallest peak in the Laurentians. The chairlift to the top (one of 13) operates all year, except during high winds, and views are breathtaking. The 94 marked ski trails range from easy to double black diamond.

The inns, shops, and steep-roofed houses of the lakeside village retain the charm of years gone by, with nary a franchise in sight. Accessible via the nearby airport, the lake stretches fjord-like 12km/7.5mi up the valley, and small craft and windsurfing gear can be rented. Just steps from the lifts, Station Mont-Tremblant resort *(819-681-2000 or 888-738-1777. www.tremblant.ca)*, is a state-of-the-art walking village with 2,000 rooms in hotels and condos, along with shops, restaurants and resort services. In warmer months, golf is the main activity, on two nearby courses.

Sainte-Adèle★

The Laurentian Autoroute *(Autoroute 15)* twists up into the Laurentians, and the older road, Highway 117, executes even more turns on the way north, past mountains still forested or turned into ski resorts. Sainte-Adèle *(Exit 67)*, set around a small lake, offers nearby slopes to suit differing tastes. **Côtes 40-80** (Hill 40-80) is an unpretentious set of moderate runs with an old-time air, and some old equipment, including rope tows. At the higher end is **Le Chantecler** *(450-229-3555)* encompassing several peaks and a ski-in-ski-out hotel.

Sainte-Marguerite-du-Lac-Masson★

12km/7mi northeast of Sainte-Adèle via Hwy. 370.

The Laurentian lake district begins at Sainte-Adèle, where the Canadian Shield refuses to drain water into the ground. Sainte-Marguerite on Lake Masson is one of the first traditional summer lake resorts in the mountains.

Saint-Sauveur-des-Monts★

60km/37mi northwest of Montreal via Autoroute 15 north to Exit 60.

Saint-Sauveur marks the major ski area closest to Montreal. Mont St-Sauveur and Mont-Avila *(450-227-4671 or 514-871-0101; www.montsaintsauveur.com)*, just off Autoroute 15 at kilometre 60, are jointly operated, with interconnecting trails. St-Sauveur has a maximum 230m/700ft drop, 38 trails, and extremely fast chairlifts that pack the skiers onto the slopes. Mont-Avila has a tube slide in addition to ski trails. Once the snow's gone, water slides and pools keep visitors coming. The huge wooden Mont St-Sauveur ski lodge was considered a landmark building when it opened in 1977.

Ski Under the Stars

For a quick escape, drive 40 minutes up to Saint-Sauveur on a late winter afternoon, and buy a reduced-rate ticket for **night skiing**. Ski traffic is lighter than during the day, and the slopes are well lit for an adventure that can be enjoyed in relatively few resorts. You'll be back in Montreal by bedtime.

West Island and Beyond★★

West of downtown Montreal. Métro Lionel-Groulx, then bus 211 (221 rush hour) to Sainte-Anne; or train from Windsor Station.

It's called *L'Ouest de l'Île* in French, or more usually *Le West-Island*, in recognition of the English-speaking character of this part of Montreal. Bedroom suburbs take up much of the terrain, but a number of formerly independent towns preserve their heritage architecture. **Lachine** is the terminus of the **Lachine Canal★★**, site of the **Fur Trade Museum★** *(see Museums)*. You can visit most of these sites in an easy half-day excursion by municipal bus.

Pointe-Claire★

22km/14mi west of Montreal via Autoroute 20 to Exit 50.

Little shops filled with antiques, the tearoom and coffee shop without a recognised brand name, the village florist and the inn weren't put in place for tourists. They've survived the winds of change that have sent shoppers and businesses to the malls in other suburbs, and they've flourished among clients who appreciate good taste. Get off the bus where it turns from Avenue Cartier onto Lakeshore *(Bord-du-Lac)*, and take time to stroll Pointe-Claire's quiet streets and browse the village shops.

Pointe-Claire's pretty **windmill** survives from 1709, when its solid wall provided refuge during attacks by Natives. The nearby convent dates from 1867, the Church of St. Joachim to 1882.

Stroll eastward along Lakeshore Road to appreciate the superb river views and the substantial houses that face the water. Past Boulevard St-Jean is **Stewart Hall★**, a half-scale replica of a Scottish Manor, now used as a cultural centre.

Sainte-Anne-de-Bellevue★

34km/21mi west of Montreal via Autoroute 20 to Exit 39.

A mixed English- and French-speaking village, Sainte-Anne fills up in summer when visitors seek its waterside cafes and offbeat shops. An old set of locks still provides safe passage from the Ottawa River into the St. Lawrence. **Sainte-Anne Church** (1853) occupies the site of the 1703 chapel where fur traders prayed before undertaking the perilous trip to the west. The **Simon Fraser House** *(153 Rue Ste-Anne)* was inhabited by the legendary Scots trader until his death in 1839, and now houses a cafe. Characterized by its massive stone foundations, **Hudson Bay House** *(9 Rue Ste-Anne)* served variously as a trading post, a Mounties' barracks and a hotel.

Sainte-Anne-de-Bellevue Canal National Historic Site – Once part of a busy inland shipping route to Ottawa and the Great Lakes, the canal now mostly sees pleasure boats, and occasionally an organized cruise *(www.pc.gc.ca/lhn-nhs/qc/annedebellevue; 450-447-4888)*.

Sainte Anne Surroundings – Located on Rue Ste-Anne, McGill University's agricultural school occupies the **Macdonald Campus**. You can visit the extensive collection of the **Lyman Entomological Museum** *(open Mon–Fri 9am–5pm; 514-398-7914)*. **Morgan Arboretum** is the university's forest reserve, home to over 200 bird species. It's a favoured cross-country ski area in winter *(150 Chemin des Pins off Chemin Sainte-Marie; 514-398-7811; www.morganarboretum.org; open daily 9am–4pm, grounds open until sunset; $5 to walk, $6 to ski)*.

Île Perrot

45km/28mi west of Montreal via Autoroute 20.

Just off the western end of Montreal, this island is still partially rural, and retains vestiges of the French regime.

Church of St. Jeanne of Chantal★
(Église Sainte-Jeanne-de-Chantal) – Rue de l'Église, Village-sur-le-Lac (south sector of island), 514-453-2125. http://pages.infinit.net/eglisejc. Open for tours by appointment only, Jul–Aug Mon–Fri 10am–5pm, weekends 9am–5pm. This late 18C stone church recalls rural life before Île Perrot was a suburb of Montreal. Early 19C sculptures by Joseph Turcaut and Louis-Xavier Leprohon remain inside.

Pointe-du-Moulin Historic Park★
(Parc historique Pointe-du-Moulin) – 500 Boul. Don-Quichotte. 514-453-5936. www.pointedumoulin.com. Open mid-May–Aug 9am–8pm, Sept–early Oct weekends 9am–6pm. $3, ($5 weekends). A restored mill is in working operation. Exhibits in the miller's house illustrate the rural way of life in New France, including old-fashioned breadmaking. Views stretch to the distant Adirondack mountains in New York State.

Vaudreuil-Dorion

50km/31mi west of Montreal via Autoroute 20.

The first municipality on the mainland retains grand houses from the colonial period.

Trestler House★ (Maison Trestler) – 85 Chemin de la Commune, Dorion. 450-455-6920. www.trestler.qc.ca. $4. Open Mon–Fri 10am–noon & 1pm–4pm, weekends 1pm–4pm. Follow Rue St-Henri north from Autoroute 20, then Rue Trestler east. This great stone mansion was erected by a Hessian mercenary who came out on the losing side in the American Revolution but ended up a winner in Canada. Johan-Josef (later Jean-Joseph) Trestler, like many of his comrades in arms, integrated into the French-Canadian community. He established a combination fur trading outpost/general store/mansion/fortress. Some rooms still sport 18C and 19C furnishings.

Lanaudière

Generations of Montrealers have gone northeast to Lanaudière to fish, hunt, and listen to beautiful music in quintessentially French-Canadian villages where the forests of the Canadian Shield begin.

Joliette★

75km/46mi from Montreal by Autoroute 40 & Autoroute 31.

Musicians of world renown perform at the **Festival International de Lanaudière** *(Jun–late Aug)* in an amphitheatre in the woods, and in the churches of Quebec's summer cultural capital.

Joliette Art Museum (Musée d'art de Joliette) – *145 Rue Wilfrid-Corbeil. 450-756-0311. www.musee.joliette.org. Open Jun–Aug Tue–Sun 11am–5pm. Rest of the year Wed–Sun noon–5pm. $4.* This premier Quebec museum displays early works reflecting a vision of God adapted to a remote colony, as well as paintings by modern artists.

Cathedral – *2 Rue St-Charles Borromée Nord. Open year-round Tue–Fri 11:30am–3:30pm, weekends 2pm–5pm.* A domed Romanesque structure, the cathedral showcases vaults and columns worthy of the great cities of Europe as well as polished wood floors characteristic of Quebec.

From Joliette, wind along Highway 131. The fabled spring thaw brings out the best of the **Seven Falls of Saint-Zénon★**, 20km/12mi past Sainte-Émélie-de-l'Énergie *(450-884-0484; www.haute-matawinie.com; open mid-May–Nov daily 9:30am–6pm; $4.50).* Be sure to see **Bridal Veil Falls** *(Voile de la mariée)* in May; once the 60m/197ft falls dry up in June, the hiking is even better.

The South Shore★   *Rive-Sud/Montérégie*

Reaching away from Montreal through suburbs and flat, fertile farmland, the south bank of the St. Lawrence River appears to be broken by stranded little mountains, the **Monteregian Hills**. The hills provide great opportunities for sport and pleasure, all within sight of Montreal's landmarks.

Fort Blunder

Upriver from Fort Lennox National Historic Site are the remains of what came to be called Fort Blunder, on the shores of Lake Champlain. The American outpost was abandoned when its garrison discovered it was on the wrong side of the border.

Fort Chambly National Historic Site★★
Lieu historique national du Canada du Fort-Chambly

30km/19mi south of Montreal via Autoroute 10 east, then north on Hwy. 133. 2 Rue de Richelieu, Chambly. 450-658-1585. www.pc.gc.ca. Open Apr–mid-May Wed–Sun 10am–5pm, mid-May–Aug daily 10am–5pm, Sept–Oct Wed–Sun 10am–5pm. $5.

Roam the solid old stone ramparts of Fort Chambly—the only fortification that remains from the French regime—and imagine the British on their way from the colony of New York in their quest to conquer New France. Artifacts and exhibitions re-create garrison life during the French regime.

Nearby is the 1812 **guardhouse,** dating from the British era, when the threat came from the Americans.

Fort Lennox National Historic Site★
Lieu historique national du Canada du Fort-Lennox

60km/38mi south of Montreal via Take Autoroute 10 east to Autoroute 35 south to St-Jean-sur-Richelieu; then Rte. 233 south to St-Paul-de-l'Île aux Noix. 450-291-5700. www.pc.gc.ca. Open mid-May–mid-Jun Mon–Fri 10am–5pm, weekends 10am–6pm; mid-Jun–Aug daily 10am–6pm; Sept–mid-Oct weekends 10am–6pm. $6, including ferry.

Île aux Noix (Walnut Island) is the site of this 19C star-shaped British defensive work, state-of-the-art for its day and surrounded by a moat. Fort Lennox was completed in 1829, just in time for an easing of tension with the Americans, and no angry shot was ever fired from its bastions. Ride the **ferry** to visit the fort, and appreciate its strategic setting guarding the river.

Barracks, guardhouse and **officers' quarters** are ordered and symmetrical, mirroring inflexible British field tactics and formations.

St-Lambert and the Seaway

Opposite Parc Jean-Drapeau. Métro Longueuil, then bus 1 to Écluse (Lock); or Autoroute 20 service road to the sign for Écluse.

Head out to St-Lambert for an up-close view of operations on the St. Lawrence Seaway, the set of embankments, canals, and **locks★** that allow ocean ships to sail past Montreal and onward to the Great Lakes. Just beyond the locks, you can watch the two sections of the **Victoria Bridge★** rise and fall to allow Seaway and motorized traffic to move continuously. You won't see an equivalent feat of engineering unless you go all the way to Panama.

The venues listed below were selected for their ambience, location and/or value for money. Rates indicate the average cost of an appetizer, a main course and a dessert for one person (not including tax, gratuity or beverages). Most restaurants are open daily and accept major credit cards. Call for information regarding reservations, dress code and opening hours. Restaurants listed are located in Montreal unless otherwise noted. For a complete listing of restaurants in this guide, see Index.

$$$$ over $75	**$$ $25–$50**
$$$ $50–$75	**$ less than $25**

Eating in French – An *entrée* in French is what you have when you begin your dining experience—an "appetizer" or "starter" on the English side of the menu. *Le plat principal* usually goes by the name of "main course" in English. Breakfast, lunch, and dinner in French Canada are *le petit dejeuner, le dîner,* and *le souper*; no translation is required for *le dessert. Table d'hôte* refers to a fixed-price menu, which may change daily.

Luxury

The Beaver Club $$$$ English

900 Boul. René-Lévesque Ouest, in Fairmont The Queen Elizabeth hotel. Closed Sun. 514-861-3511. www.fairmont.com.

Lair of early Montreal's fur-trade tycoons, the Beaver Club now carries on in beautiful beamed brick premises. Traditional English roast beef, rack of suckling pig and caribou rosettes are mainstays, but everything is prepared with French savoir-faire—the grilled steak comes with red wine butter, the calf's liver is glazed with sherry vinegar and honey. Jacket and tie requested.

La Queue de Cheval $$$$ American

1221 Boul. René-Lévesque West, 514-390-0090. www.queuedecheval.com.

When is an American-style steak-and-seafood house controversial? When it opens in a city that already has more than its share of fine cuisine establishments. When it's huge and elegant and demonstrates that American beef, exquisitely prepared, can rival European fare for the attention of the educated palate. Appetizers shine, from an assortment of sausages with mustard to classic steak tartare; try an assortment of these instead of a main course.

Toqué! $$$$ French

900 Place Jean-Paul Riopelle, near Victoria Square. Closed Sun & Mon. 514-499-0292.
www.restaurant-toque.com.

Toqué! is invariably mentioned among the best and most innovative of Montreal restaurants. The journey from the kitchen of chef Normand Laprise to your plate can involve detours to Japan, the Arctic, or the tropics to yield a

complexity of tastes never imagined: Nova
Scotia scallops with cranberries and apple
mousse, tuna tartare with sprouts and jalapeño
cream, salmon with citrus, red squash-and-
parmesan risotto with market vegetables (for
the vegetarian). Tasting menus with or without
wine eliminate the dilemma of what to choose.
All this is served in futuristic premises of glass,
steel and sleek lines.

Chez La Mère Michel $$$ French

1209 Rue Guy. 514-934-0473. Closed Sun. www.chezlameremichel.com

"Mother Michael" has been steadfast for almost forty years in an elegant gray-stone town house. The dining rooms are formal, with upholstered chairs, paintings, and murals. And the menu will hold no surprises for those familiar with the best of Paris—magret of duck, lamb in pastry, or lamb, beef and veal medallions in three sauces—except, perhaps, for the tournedos of bison. Formal dress is appropriate here.

Chez Queux $$$ French

158 Rue St-Paul Est. 514-866-5194. www.chezqueux.com.

With its massive stone and brick walls, Chez Queux
stands out for its reliability, professional service, and
comprehensive, award-winning wine list. Classic dishes
include Dover sole, or rack of lamb with herbs, and
roast duck with wild berries.

Ferreira Café
$$$ Portuguese

1446 Rue Peel. Closed Sun. 514-848-0988. www.ferreiracafe.com.

Opening this restaurant in downtown Montreal was a dream-come-true for Portugal native Carlos Ferreira. True to his roots, Ferreira presents the ambience and cuisine of his country in the Mediterranean-style trattoria. Locals, celebrities and visiting dignitaries—including the President of Portugal in 2001—all flock to sample Portuguese and continental fare such as gazpacho with lobster and coriander; seafood Cataplana; and cod with olive oil and tomato compote. Racking up some 60,000 bottles, the extensive wine list includes a good selection of white, tawny and vintage ports.

Laloux
$$$ Contemporary French

250 Ave. des Pins Est. 514-287-9127. www.laloux.com.

Laloux is much sought after for its surprising nouvelle cuisine, anything from vegetable tartare in gazpacho or monkfish pops with eggplant caviar to a Burgundian crêpe with duck confit. There is also a fine assortment of wines paired with local cheeses. Large windows and mirrors suggest an establishment on a Parisian boulevard, rather than humble surroundings near Rue St-Denis.

La Tour de Ville
$$$ International

777 Rue University. Sun, brunch only. Closed Mon. 514-879-4777. www.deltahotels.com

The name's a play on words (*tour* is turn, tour, and tower) that tells everything: this is Montreal's only revolving restaurant, atop the tower of the Delta Centre-Ville Hotel. In the course of the evening you'll enjoy the spectacular sweep of the city—from the mountains to the Montreal Tower—for at least a spin and a half. It's also a culinary tour, as the cuisine consists of buffets with regional themes—Italian, Japanese, Mediterranean, and more. For a daytime view, try the Sunday brunch.

Les Caprices de Nicolas
$$$ French

2072 Rue Drummond. 514-282-9790. www.lescaprices.com.

Montreal's most romantic restaurant offers secluded corners, as well as a cheery greenhouse-like interior garden. The fine French cuisine emphasizes interesting presentations with local ingredients. Offerings may include roast venison with chestnut chips, duck breast with pear chutney, or Arctic char poached in coriander oil.

Les Remparts
$$$ French-Canadian

93 Rue de la Commune. 514-392-1649. www.restaurantlesremparts.com.

Tucked into the basement of the Auberge du Vieux-Port, with its stone walls and low, beamed ceiling, Les Remparts (The Ramparts) suggests New France. The preparation is French-style, adapted to the availability of fresh

ingredients. Signature appetizers are grilled
quail with honey and sesame oil, and terrine
of braised duck and foie gras; main courses
include venison seared with foie gras, guinea
hen supreme, and suckling pig. A full traditional Quebec-style dinner will be cooked
up for holidays. Open daily for dinner, week-
days for lunch.

Restaurant St-Amable $$$ French

410 Place Jacques-Cartier, 514-866-3471. www.st-amable.com.

Of many restaurants with terraces on Place Jacques-Cartier, the St-Amable, set
in an 18C fortress house redolent of New France, is one of the more reliable.
The offerings are all familiar French-style classics, from Dijon snails to start, to
mains courses of Châteaubriand and beef in peppercorn sauce. A lower-price
table d'hôte menu is also available.

Zen $$$ Chinese

1050 Rue Sherbrooke Ouest. 514-499-0801. www.omnihotels.com.

Zen creates its own book of the Orient, starting with a sleek Art Moderne
environment of curving, unembellished surfaces, and tables set on stages.
Service is anything but traditional Chinese-style; a number of dishes will be
sliced, diced and rolled up at tableside, with a French flourish. The nouvelle
Chinese menu builds on Szechuan cooking, with contributions from elsewhere
in Asia: an exotic warm salad, fish with seaweed, and the mainstay Peking duck
and General Tao chicken. For true adventure and freedom of choice, a fixed-
price dinner allows unlimited selections from the menu.

Moderate

Boris Bistro $$ French

465 Rue McGill. Closed Sun. Mon lunch only. 514-848-9575. www.borisbistro.com.

Boris—mascot as well as restaurant—has a loyal following of professionals in
Old Montreal who bring their friends back into the city for dinner. Delightful
tavern fare in gleaming surroundings emphasizes *le terroir*—fine regional
products, such as venison sausage, wild mushroom fricassée or braised rabbit,
when available—along with variations on classics like duck confit and buffalo
steak-frites. The outdoor patio is a dramatic work of urban archaeology in
itself, exposing the frame and walls of a building-that-was.

Chez l'Epicier $$ French

311 St-Paul Est. 514-878-2232. www.chezlepicier.com.

This restaurant and wine bar is also, literally, "The Grocer's," with tables set
among shelves and in front of counters stocked with delicacies from Quebec
and all over. The fare is creative: parmesan-oil ravioli on duck confit with wild
mushrooms, followed by halibut marinated in ginger with a caviar of salmon,
mango and chives. On a warm day, carry a terrine out to a bench by the Old Port.

Hélène de Champlain $$ French-Canadian

200 Tour d l'Île, Île Ste-Hélène. 514-395-2424. www.helenedechamplain.com.

The city of Montreal's very own island mansion is available to impress everyone when it's not hosting visiting dignitaries. Stone walls, beamed ceilings, massive fireplaces, balconies, and armoires suggest the ruling class of New France in Jean-Drapeau Park opposite downtown. Offerings are mainly French-style seafood appetizers and elaborate presentations of fowl and meat: breast of duck with raspberry vinegar, breaded veal with hazelnut and gorgonzola sauce.

L'Académie $$ Italian

4051 Rue St-Denis. 514-849-2249. www.lacademie.ca. Métro Sherbrooke.

At L'Académie, gleaming chrome, spare lines, and floor-to-ceiling glass suggest a contemporary Roman bistro, as does the menu. Gnocchi with gorgonzola sauce and veal scallops in mustard sauce—along with low prices—attract customers who line up, bottle of wine in hand. The *table d'hôte* proposes a specialty of the day, such as swordfish with avocado salsa.

Le Parchemin $$ French

1333 Rue University. 514-844-1619. www.leparchemin.com.

A former parish house for Christ Church Cathedral, Le Parchemin exemplifies creative architectural recycling. It's an updated period piece, with elegant dining rooms fitted with wainscoting, and decorated with paintings and large antiques. Specialties include marinated duck with orange peel, marinated bison, and the sinful *iles flottantes* (floating islands) for dessert. A tasting menu is also available. The daily lunch special, including wine or beer, may not be the chef at his most elegant, but it does introduce the restaurant at a bargain price.

Le Petit Moulinsart $$ Belgian

139 Rue St-Paul Ouest. 514-843-7432. www.lepetitmoulinsart.com.

Step into a corner of Brussels at this little restaurant with its bistro chairs, gleaming light-wood panelling, waiters in bow ties, and pictures that pay homage to Tintin, Belgium's most famous comic-character export. The specialty is mussels, and everything else on the menu is authentic, too, right down to the beers, Belgian fries, veal à la Rodenbach, and at times horsemeat steak (of which Canada is a major exporter) topped with cheese.

Le Taj
$$ Indian

2077 Rue Stanley. 514-845-9015. www.restaurantletaj.com.

The décor may be generic, but the food is genuine Northern Indian, and attracts a following of businessmen, professors, and politicians who know good value. The specialty is marinated meats cooked in a tandoor (a traditional clay oven), and there's a good assortment of curries. Plates of fresh, hot *nan* bread go perfectly with excellent mulligatawny soup. The lunchtime buffet is a special value; all items are from the menu, with no starchy or fried fillers.

Macao
$$ French

2070 Rue St-Denis. 514-223-6411. Métro Berri-UQAM.

The surroundings in the Latin Quarter are relaxed, but the French cuisine is as refined as in many a more chic establishment. The fixed-price dinner includes four courses, with seasonal specialties like seafood ravioli with saffon-and-ginger sauce, duck breast stew with port and raspberry sauce, and buffalo with garlic confit. Bring your own wine to make a bargain even more so.

Magnan
$$ Steakhouse

2602 Rue St-Patrick. 514-935-9647. www.magnanresto.com.

This cavernous tavern near Atwater Market speaks in working-class tones, with plywood panelling, photos of local celebrities, and hearty fare. And the patrons speak both languages, switching effortlessly from unaccented English to unaccented French. Roast beef and steaks are mainstays, and, depending on the season, you might also find mussels, salmon, or surprisingly low-priced lobster. The beer is cheap, and much of it is consumed upstairs while watching hockey and football on television.

Restaurant Julien
$$ French

1191 Rue Union. 514-871-1581. www.restaurantjulien.com.

Here's an Old Montreal-style restaurant in an uptown setting, with tall glass windows and cozy banquettes. The food style is French, but the flavours come from everywhere, as in sautéed vegetables and tofu flavoured with cilantro, sesame-perfumed red tuna pizza, and roast guinea fowl perfumed with tarragon. The lunchtime *table d'hôte* is a good value.

Restaurant du Vieux-Port
$$ Contemporary

39 Rue St-Paul Est. 514-866-3175. www.restaurantduvieuxport.com.

A one-time sailors' inn, the Vieux-Port is a no-pretense, reliable steak and chop house, serving customers in numerous rooms with exposed stone walls. You'll find chicken breast with shrimp and garlic spinach, filet mignon with mushroom ragoût, and grilled salmon, but you won't find a subdued atmosphere. People come here to relax and gab over good food.

Stash Café
$$ Polish

200 Rue St-Paul Ouest. 514-845-6611. www.stashcafe.com.

With 30 years at the same Old Montreal location, Stash has outlasted the competition with excellent Polish cuisine. The fare is expectedly hearty: borscht (beet soup topped with sour cream) to start, *bigos* (meat-and-sausage stew), pierogi (dumplings), and stuffed cabbage as main courses, and dark—really dark—brown bread on the side. For a real Polish feast, enjoy the complete wild boar dinner in season—perfect on a winter night. The stone surroundings are pure Old Montreal, but you could easily imagine yourself in a castle near the Baltic.

Inexpensive

Basha
$ Lebanese

930 Rue Ste-Catherine Ouest, upstairs. 514-866-4272.

This Lebanese fast-food firm has numerous outlets around central Montreal, in and out of the Underground City and mini-malls. At this location, you get an excellent choice of kebabs, salads and vegetarian spreads, such as hummus served with pita, for very little money—plus a ringside seat to watch all the goings-on on busy Rue Sainte-Catherine below.

Beauty's
$ American

93 Ave. Mt-Royal Ouest. Open Mon–Fri until 4pm, Sat & Sun until 5pm. 514-849-8883. www.beautys.ca.

It's all about chutzpah. Give them a retro diner, slide them an omelet and fries or a bagel smeared with cream cheese, chopped liver or salmon, top off the coffee, toss the check at them, and bring on the next patrons before the first ones can vacate their seats. Montrealers have been loving the uncouth service here for years.

Café Santropol
$ Canadian

3990 Rue St Urbain, 514-842-3110. Métro Saint-Laurent and bus 55. www.santropol.com.

The dream has never faded at Café Santropol, a sixties alternative café now in gracious middle age. The hammered-tin ceiling was antique when the place began, and everything is just a bit more worn and comfortable with each new year. Enjoy tall cheese, fruit and nut sandwiches on brown bread along with thick soups and fruit shakes. Part of what you pay goes to support a meals-on-wheels program.

Deer Garden
$ Asian

1162 Boul. St-Laurent. 514-861-1056.

It's a good thing that the food is so good at the Deer Garden *(Jardin du Cerf)*, because nobody bothered much with the luncheonette-style décor. You'll find a jumble of plates from all over Asia, including Szechuan shrimp, Cantonese sautéed beef, and Thai chicken in pepper sauce. Aside from the excellence of the food, another plus is that you may bring your own bottle of wine.

Frites Alors $ Belgian

1710 Rue St-Denis (and other locations). 514-842-9905. www.fritealors.com.

The Belgian fries are so good that it's practically all they have, with an assortment of sauces, but you can add protein to your lunch with merguez sausages,
a hamburger, or horsemeat tartare.

Jardin du Nord $ Chinese

80 Rue de la Gauchetière Ouest. 514-395-8023.

Chinatown's pedestrians-only main street is restaurant row, and Jardin du Nord
is one of the better eateries. Choose among main courses such as Szechuan
beef, chicken with walnuts, and crispy beef. Check out the menu posted in the
window, and if you don't see what you like, look across the street at **Nan Pic**
(75A Rue de la Gauchetière; 514-395-8016), where the fare is northern and the
gourmet menu offers mango shrimp and crispy spinach with chicken.

La Brioche Lyonnaise $ French

1593 Rue St-Denis. 514-842-7017.

Here's a slice of Paris on Rue Saint-Denis: wonderful
sandwiches on fresh baguettes, salads, crêpes in
many varieties, and acres of brioches and other
desserts to choose from in the display cases.

La Cabane Grecque $ Greek

102 Rue Prince-Arthur Est. 514-849-0122. www.lacabanegrecque.com.

The competition is fierce among the Greek restaurants along lively Prince
Arthur, to everyone's benefit. La Cabane Grecque is just one of numerous
establishments that offer a soup-to-dessert meal for under $25, and for half
that amount at lunch. Choose from moussaka, steak, roast chicken, and shish
kebabs. The quality and quantity of food, considering the price, are surprising.
And that's not all. If you bring your own bottle wine, the waiter will uncork
and serve it at no additional charge.

Le Commensal $ Vegetarian

1204 Ave. McGill College. 514-871-1480. 1720 Rue St-Denis, 514-845-2627.

It's a cafeteria set-up, but the several outlets of the Commensal chain serve
vegetarian *haute cuisine* to rival the fare in conventional restaurants. There's
no need for translation. Choose your courses in exactly the quantities you
wish, pay by weight, and sit down to enjoy. Terrines, lasagnas and vegetable
chili have a wide following, and are also available in supermarkets.

Première Moisson $ French

Atwater Market, Métro Lionel Groulx. 514-932-0328. www.premieremoisson.com.

This chain of bakery/pastry shops has many outlets, but the most enticing is the
location on the upper level of Atwater Market, where there's ample terrace-style
seating in all seasons. Fill up on pastries, quiches, chocolatines, and sausages, or just
linger over a cup of coffee. Afterwards, wander past the nearby vendors' stalls and
sample cheeses, patés, terrines, and spices from around the world.

Schwartz's Deli

$ Delicatessen

3895 Boul. St-Laurent. 514-842-4813. www.schwartzsdeli.com.

Jewish-style cuisine is *not* the same everywhere. One of Montreal's specialties is smoked meat, with a flavour achieved by secret blends of spices and the characteristic smoke of local hardwoods. It's served piled on rye bread, and nowhere so generously and with such renown as at Charcuterie Hebraique Schwartz's.

3 Amigos

$ Mexican

1657 Rue Ste-Catherine Ouest. 514-939-3329.

This house of excellent Mexican food has many more than three amigos. Portions of tostadas, enchiladas, quesadillas and chimichangas are large and attractively prepared with bounteous salad and rice on the side. Doggie bags are a common sight, along with hungry students from nearby Concordia University who recognise a good deal. Go Wednesday for half-priced fajitas, or Sunday for cheap tacos.

Tim Hortons

$ Canadian

48 Rue Notre-Dame Est. 514-875-4540. www.timhortons.com. Also 159 Rue St-Antoine Ouest, 514-871-1509, 605 Boul. René-Lévesque Ouest, 514-395-1207 and other locations.

What brings Canadians together across vast distances, assorted languages, extremes of climate and inter-provincial bickering? It's the soups, sandwiches, donuts, and above all the coffee served at Tim Hortons, the chain of gleaming, quick-serve eateries—named for a hockey great—that exemplify wholesome and unpretentious Canadian food. Combinations are filling, nutritious and a great value.

Quebec City

Luxury

Le Saint-Amour

$$$$ French

48 Rue Ste-Ursule. 418-694-0667. www.saint-amour.com.

For a quarter-century, chef Jean-Luc Boulay has been leading the way in merging regional ingredients from Quebec with the classic cooking methods of France. Caribou steak with juniper berries, foie gras of Quebec duck prepared six ways, or salmon tartare and snow crab with avocado mousse may appear on the menu, along with filet mignon or lobster. Your choice of dining areas includes the Winter Garden, a high-ceilinged, Victorian conservatory.

L'Astral

$$$ French

Hotel Le Concorde, 1225 Cours du General-de-Montcalm. 418-647-2222. www.lastral.com.

If there's a city made for viewing from a variety of vantage points, it's Quebec. L'Astral offers a great viewpoint, in a revolving restaurant atop Hôtel Le Concorde. The byways of the Old City and the valley of the St. Lawrence spread before you, in an ever-changing panorama. All this comes with fine French cooking, such as filet mignon in an aubergine crust. Watching your pennies? Go for the lunch buffet or the early-bird dinner.

Laurie Raphaël $$$ French

117 Rue Dalhousie. 418-692-4555. www.laurieraphael.com.

On the outside, Laurie Raphaël is a contemporary glass pavilion attached to a modern building, but inside, it's Quebec City's premier adventurous gourmet establishment, a world music of cuisine with a solid French base. Chef Daniel Vézina's changing menu features artisanal Quebecois products such as smoked salmon and emu from the Charlevoix region.

Restaurant Initiale $$$ Contemporary

54 rue St-Pierre. Closed Sun. 418-694-1818. www.restaurantinitiale.com.

Worthy of a special occasion, Initiale cossets diners in a sleek, soothing space in Lower Town. Chef Yves Lebrun's delectable contemporary cuisine will tantalize your taste buds whether you stick to the à la carte menu or go with one of the nightly tastings. Regional Canadian products marry with French technique and a dash of innovation, resulting in the likes of pan-fried foie gras with pomegranate juice, quince confit and armillaire mushrooms; or hake filet with corn and orange, napped with curry sauce.

Restaurant L'Échaudé $$$ French

73 Rue Sault-au-Matelot. 418-692-1299. www.echaude.com.

Plates are served as they would be in Paris, in a setting fitted with light-coloured wainscoting and decorated generously with plants. Inventive takes on classics include medallions of venison with wild berry sauce, duck confit, and grilled steak with a mango sauce. A lunch menu and inclusive dinner menu are available.

Moderate

Café du Monde $$ French

84 Rue Dalhousie. 418-692-4455. www.lecafedumonde.com.

The premier locale for river gazing in all seasons is upstairs in the modern cruise terminal, where Café du Monde fuses bistro décor with huge expanses of glass. The food all smacks of French bistro fare with a local take: black pudding and duck confit are mainstays, along with venison brochette with berries; all of which goes down well on a frosty day.

47ème Parallèle $$ International

333 Rue St-Amable. 418-692-4747.

"International" is often shorthand for plain food, but not here. Try braised chicken with fruit couscous, braised boar on mushroom fricassé with truffle sauce, or tempura tuna steak with hoison sauce. The new uptown setting has a sleek ambience, with outdoor garden seating when weather permits.

Le Lapin Sauté $$ French

52 rue Petit-Champlain. 418-692-5325. www.lapinsaute.com.

Old Country charm awaits at this tiny restaurant in the historic heart of Lower Town. In the cozy dining room, dried herbs hang from the beamed ceiling and a cozy fire warms the room when it's cold outside. As the name suggests, comfort food here centers on the signature ingredient—rabbit—in the form of everything from rabbit rillettes to rabbit pie. The shady stone terrace, surrounded by leafy greenery, makes a perfect den in summer.

Portofino $$ Italian

54 Rue Couilliard. 418-692-8888. www.portofino.qc.ca.

For informal and reliable dining on familiar and well-prepared Italian specialties, Portofino is there, with pizzas cooked in a wood-burning oven—a Quebec specialty—an assortments of pastas, as well as classic veal dishes. Prices are reasonable, the atmosphere is relaxed, and you can watch the food being prepared in the open kitchen.

Voo-Doo Grill $$ Asian

575 Grande Allée. 418-647-2000. www.voodoogrill.com.

 It's all about the food *and* style *and* presentation at the Voo-Doo Grill. Dark hardwood fittings, tropical plants, and oversized statuary create the air of an eccentric's mansion somewhere in Southeast Asia. Tandoori shrimp, grain-fed citrus chicken with "volcano" sauce, and grilled wild salmon with lobster sauce are house mainstays.

Inexpensive

L'Ardoise $ Belgian

71 Rue St-Paul. 418-694-0213. www.lardoiseresto.com.

The wood panelling and café chairs at L'Ardoise in the Lower Town are a slice of Brussels, and so are the *moules-frites* (mussels and fries). Select your favorite dipping sauces and dive right in.

Le Cochon Dingue $ French-Canadian

46 Boul. Champlain. 418-692-2013. www.cochondingue.com.

 In Lower Town, where formal eateries flourish, the Cochon Dingue ("Crazy Pig") is anything but stuffy. Locals come here to feast on breakfast panini, classic steak-frites, *poutine* (a Quebecois specialty: French fries topped with cheese curds and brown gravy), and *tourtes*. Kids get their own menu.

Must Eat: Restaurants by Theme

Another Way to Look at It: Restaurants by Theme

In the preceding pages we've organized the restaurants by price category; here we've arranged them by theme to help you plan your meals. Whether you're looking for a casual bite among locals or a wallet-emptying seven-course dinner at one of Canada's finest restaurants, Montreal and Quebec City have just the place for you.

Breakfast Spots
Beauty's *(p 108)*
Tim Hortons *(p 110)*
Le Cochon Dingue *(p 112)*

Easy on the Budget
Le Taj *(p 107)*
Basha *(p 108)*
Café Santropol *(p 108)*
Deer Garden *(p 108)*
Jardin du Nord *(p 109)*
La Brioche Lyonnaise *(p 109)*
La Cabane Grecque *(p 109)*
Le Commensal *(p 109)*
3 Amigos *(p 110)*

Ethnic Experiences
Ferreira Café *(p 104)*
Zen *(p 105)*
L'Académie *(p 106)*
Le Petit Moulinsart *(p 106)*
Le Taj *(p 107)*
Basha *(p 108)*
Deer Garden *(p 108)*
Stash Café *(p 108)*
Jardin du Nord *(p 109)*
La Cabane Grecque *(p 109)*
Schwartz's Deli *(p 110)*
3 Amigos *(p 110)*
Portofino *(p 112)*
Voo-Doo Grill *(p 112)*

French Cuisine
La Queue de Cheval *(p 102*
Chez La Mère Michel *(p 103)*
Chez Queux *(p 103)*
Les Caprices de Nicolas *(p 104)*
Les Remparts *(p 104)*
Restaurant St-Amable *(p 105)*
Le Parchemin *(p 106)*

Restaurant Julien *(p 107)*
Macao *(p 107)*
Le Saint-Amour *(p 110)*
Laurie Raphaël *(p 111)*
Restaurant L'Échaudé *(p 111)*
Le Lapin Sauté *(p 112)*

Neighbourhood Favourites
Boris Bistro *(p 105)*
Magnan *(p 107)*
Café Santropol *(p 108)*
Première Moisson *(p 109)*
Schwartz's Deli *(p 110)*

Places to Eat with Kids
Restaurant du Vieux-Port *(p 107)*
Beauty's *(p 108)*
Frites Alors *(p 109)*
Tim Hortons *(p 110)*
Le Cochon Dingue *(p 112)*

Restaurants for Romance
Chez La Mère Michel *(p 103)*
Chez Queux *(p 103)*
Les Caprices de Nicolas *(p 104)*
Les Remparts *(p 104)*
Hélène de Champlain *(p 106)*
Restaurant L'Échaudé *(p 111)*
Le Lapin Sauté *(p 112)*

Special-Occasion Restaurants
The Beaver Club *(p 102)*
Chez Queux *(p 103)*
La Tour de Ville *(p 104)*
L'Astral *(p 110)*
Restaurant Initiale *(p 111)*

Star Chefs
Toqué! / Normand Laprise *(p 103)*
Laloux / André Bresson *(p 104)*

The properties listed below were selected for their ambience, location and/or value for money. Prices reflect the average cost for a standard double room for two people (not including applicable taxes). Hotels in Montreal often offer special discount packages. Price ranges do not include the Canadian hotel tax, or the sales tax of 14%. Properties are located in Montreal, unless otherwise specified. For a complete list of hotels mentioned in this guide, see Index.

$$$$$	**over $350**	**$$**	**$100–$175**
$$$$	**$250–$350**	**$**	**less than $100**
$$$	**$175–$250**		

Luxury

Hôtel Le Germain $$$$$ 101 rooms

2050 Rue Mansfield. 514-849-2050 or 877-333-2050. www.hotelgermain.com.

This office building/boutique hotel oozes refined luxury. Oriental minimalism prevails in the light-filled loft-like rooms, done in earth tones with dark wood furnishings handcrafted by local artisans. Sumptuous bedding and upscale amenities such as irons and ironing boards, CD players and daily newspapers make these some of the most sought-after rooms in the city.

Hôtel Le St-James $$$$$ 61 rooms

355 Rue St-Jacques Ouest. 514-841-3111 or 866-841-3111. www.hotellestjames.com.

The grandest of the boutique hotels of Montreal, the St-James has re-vivified the tiered Beaux-Arts Merchant Bank Building. The sumptuous two-storey grand salon with its elegant spaces and secluded nooks seamlessly incorporates the former main banking hall with hardly a whiff of its former function. Rooms—and, indeed, the entire establishment—are mansion- rather than hotel-style, with hardwood paneling, paintings, brocades, custom carpets, artwork, and marble-lined bathrooms. High tea is served in the afternoon, and the library is as much a haven as a private club. The St-James is conveniently located beside the Montreal World Trade Centre and Underground City.

Fairmont The Queen Elizabeth
$$$$ 1,039 rooms

900 Boul. René-Lévesque Ouest. 514-861-3511 or 800-257-7544. www.fairmont.com.

Office-building plain on the outside, this Queen is a bastion of tradition, style and taste inside. A warren of panelled reception rooms and refined restaurants include the fabled **Beaver Club ($$$)**; the lobby **Tea Lounge ($)** where the ceremony is performed in classic English style; and the more informal **Montréalais ($$)**. John Lennon wrote *Give Peace a Chance* in Suite 1742, but the Queen is discreet about the doings of its guests. With high-speed Internet access and a separate breakfast area, the Gold Level has its own access via a panoramic elevator running up the outside of the building.

Hilton Montréal Bonaventure
$$$$ 395 rooms

900 de La Gauchetière Ouest. 514-878-2332 or 800-267-2575. www.hiltonmontreal.com.

Anonymously set atop the Place Bonaventure shopping complex and exhibition halls, the downtown Hilton pleasantly surrounds a rooftop garden courtyard and four-season outdoor pool. Its **Le Castillon restaurant ($$$)** is an unexpected re-creation of the great hall of a chateau with a reasonably priced lunchtime buffet. The Underground City provides sheltered access to the convention centre, shopping and dining.

Hostellerie Pierre du Calvet
$$$$ 9 rooms

405 Rue Bonsecours. 514-282-1725 or 866-544-1725. www.pierreducalvet.ca.

This historic house *(see Landmarks)* has the makings of a memorable stay, in rooms with fireplaces and beamed ceilings, furnished with massive antiques and canopy beds. Uneven floors and exposed stone walls are not re-creations, but the real thing. Noted for its French cuisine and Quebec ingredients, the **Pierre du Calvet ($$$)** restaurant serves such dishes as venison paupiettes and filet mignon in its dramatic, high-ceilinged space. A lighter lunch menu is available in the adjacent **Filles du Roy ($-$$)**. The covered greenhouse patio is pleasant for breakfast, even in winter.

Hôtel Gault $$$$ 29 rooms

449 Rue Ste-Héléne. 514-904-1616 or 866-904-1616. www.hotelgault.com.

At the Gault, minimalist modern design takes centre stage against the background of an 1871 cotton importer's warehouse. Outside, the premises are ornate, inspired by the Beaux-Arts buildings of contemporary Paris. Inside, only the original cast-iron stanchions remain, contrasting with unornamented steel, concrete and white oak. Loft-like guest rooms are large and open, and decked out with designer furnishings. Consistent with partial ownership by media mogul Daniel Langlois, state-of-the-art entertainment consoles enhance each room. Rue Ste-Hélène is one of the quietest streets in Old Montreal.

Hotel InterContinental Montréal $$$$ 357 rooms

360 Rue St-Antoine Ouest. 514-987-9900 or 888-424-6835. www.ichotelsgroup.com.

Although its turrets and roof may resemble a castle, the InterContinental offers intimate spaces. It's even possible to overlook the lobby and check-in area if you're not familiar with the property, tucked behind a row of historic façades in the Montreal World Trade Centre. Carpets, upholstered chairs and fluffy linens are straight out of Paris. This is as close as you'll come to Old Montreal and still be in a full-service hotel, with a health club, convention facilities, and an all-season rooftop lap pool. **Les Continents ($$$)** serves local ingredients in French style, while **Chez Plume ($$)** in the Nordheimer annex is a relaxed bistro.

Hôtel Le Saint-Sulpice $$$$ 108 rooms

414 Rue St-Sulpice. 514-288-1000 or 877-785-7423. www.lesaintsulpice.com.

Although it was built to the scale and profile of Old Montreal, the Saint-Sulpice is a recent hotel. Rooms and public areas off the garden courtyard are flooded with natural light, and generous use of dark hardwoods and leather make an environment that's modern but still warm. All guest rooms are large suites, either with an open plan or a separate bedroom; all have a microwave. Many rooms feature fireplaces, and all have high-speed Internet connections. Try **S restaurant ($$$)** for contemporary French fare.

Hôtel Nelligan $$$$ 64 rooms

106 Rue St-Paul Ouest. 514-788-2040 or 877-788-2040. www.hotelnelligan.com.

"Nelligan" is of Irish origin, to be sure, but in Quebec, the name refers to Émile Nelligan—poet, romantic, bon-vivant, exemplar of good taste—all the qualities epitomized in this boutique hotel. Set in a 19C building, stone and brick walls establish the period atmosphere, along with dark wood furnishings and plush chairs. A former courtyard with a greenhouse roof, the atrium is bordered by grillwork and decorated with plants. Public spaces, including a library, are cozy and conducive to conversation. **Verses restaurant ($$$)** makes an elegant setting for local specialties.

Hôtel Place d'Armes
$$$$ 135 rooms

55 Saint-Jacques Ouest. 514-842-1887 or 888-450-1887. www.hotelplacedarmes.com.

Following current trends in boutique hotels, the Place d'Armes is not a restoration, but an impressive re-use of the dramatic spaces of the former Great Scottish Life Insurance Building and adjacent structures. Beaux-Arts architectural detailing serves as a background to updated Art Deco and contemporary furnishings and elements. With their exposed brick walls, rooms are at once homey and state-of-the-art, with Internet connections and large bathrooms. The rooftop terrace/bar offers wonderful views down to Place d'Armes and Old Montreal. Rainspa has Montreal's only hammam (Oriental steam bath). Breakfast and an afternoon drink are included in the rate.

Hotel St. Paul
$$$$ 120 rooms

355 Rue McGill. 514-380-2222 or 866-380-2202. www.hotelstpaul.com.

A landmark in Montreal's business district for more than a century, the Canadian Express Building is now a showcase of Modernist design, from the stunning, illuminated-from-inside alabaster lobby fireplace to rooms with white leather sofas, suspended light fixtures, and gleaming black floors. **Cube restaurant ($$$)** challenges preconceptions of how fine food should be served (think duck liver paired with a different chutney every day, goat cheese-and-walnut ravioli and sea bass with pepper-chorizo dressing).

Hotel W Montréal
$$$$ 357 rooms

901 Square-Victoria. 514-395-3100 or 888-627-7081. www.whotels.com/montreal.

Sleek W style goes perfectly with Montreal, from the spaceship lines of the Wunderbar to zen-like room and bath fittings to the cosy goose down comforters, electronic amenities and on-site spa. The financial centre and Underground City are just steps away. Dine at **Otto ($$$)** to experience a fusion of Mediterranean and exotic flavours with characteristic Quebec ingredients.

Hyatt Regency Montréal
$$$$ 606 rooms

1255 Rue Jeanne-Mance. 514-982-1234 or 800-361-8234. www.montreal.hyatt.com.

In itself, the Hyatt is a fine hotel, with numerous services and dining choices, convention facilities, indoor pool, gym, and sundeck. But what sets the Hyatt apart is its integration into the Place Desjardins commerical and office complex. Descend by elevator into the adjacent grand space for boutique browsing or festival events, and continue without stepping outside to Place des Arts, the Métro, and the convention center. Many rooms provide premier viewing for the Jazz Fest and Montreal High Lights Festival; in the hallways and restaurant you may spy the festival stars themselves.

Loews Hotel Vogue
$$$$ 142 rooms

1425 Rue de la Montagne. 514-285-5555 or 866-768-6658. www.loewshotels.com.

The Vogue is plain on the outside, as if to disguise its sumptuous interior ornamentation. While rooms are small, they are elegantly decorated with heavy curtains, silk upholstery and French provincial lamps, and have every amenity—right down to the marble-tiled bathroom with whirlpool tub. The Vogue sits near the Museum of Fine Arts and the shops along Rue Sainte-Catherine and Rue Sherbrooke.

The Ritz-Carlton Montreal $$$$ 229 rooms

1228 Rue Sherbrooke Ouest. 514-842-4212 or 800-363-0366. www.ritzmontreal.com.

For generations, the rich and powerful who have visited Montreal have stayed in this grande dame, while the local rich and powerful have held court in the public spaces. Regularly updated and impeccably maintained, the Ritz envelops its clientele in plush upholstered furniture, chandeliers and mirrors in the classic French hotel style. Full appreciation requires dinner in the **Café de Paris ($$$)** or, in mild weather, lunch in the Ritz Garden (**Jardin du Ritz; $$**) overlooking the duck pond.

Moderate

Auberge Bonaparte $$$ 31 rooms

447 Rue St-François-Xavier. 514-844-1448. www.bonaparte.com.

Here's a rare Old Montreal hotel that looks as if it's been functioning for years—in the best sense. Its attractive furnishings suggest the era of Napoleon, and its **restaurant ($$)** serves good French cuisine behind a glass storefront. Add to that a salon with fireplace, and rates that include breakfast and Internet connections in rooms individually decorated with wardrobes and large windows, and you've got a recipe for success.

Auberge de la Fontaine $$$ 21 rooms

1301 Rue Rachel Est. 514-597-0166 or 800-597-0597. www.aubergedelafontaine.com.

This urban inn has its charms, with cheerful rooms individually decorated, some with balconies and exposed brick walls. The location is peaceful, opposite La Fontaine Park, yet it's not far from Rue Saint-Denis and some of the most edgy shops and restaurants. Room rates include breakfast.

Auberge les Passants du Sans Soucy $$$ 9 rooms

171 Rue St-Paul Ouest. 514-842-2634. www.lesanssoucy.com.

The intimate Sans Soucy pioneered the revival of Old Montreal as a lodging area for visitors with refined tastes. The inn carries on its reputation with exquisite furnishings and careful attention to detail in its nine rooms, each boasting a beamed ceiling, wood floor, iron or massive wood beds, exposed stone walls, and fireplaces—not to mention modern baths, Internet connections and air conditioning. There's even an art gallery showcasing talent from the province. Breakfast is included. Reserve early.

Auberge du Vieux-Port $$$ 27 rooms

97 Rue de la Commune Est. 514-876-0081 or 888-660-7678. www.aubergeduvieuxport.com.

A one-time riverfront warehouse and general store serves as an ultra-charming setting for comfortable rooms, more relaxed in tone than at other Old Montreal boutique hotels. In the guest rooms, reproduction 18C brass bedsteads and chairs are set against exposed brick and stone walls, and sun streams in through huge windows that afford views of the St. Lawrence River on the south side. The rooftop terrace/bar is a perfect perch in mild weather. Larger loft-style accommodations are also available; all room rates includes breakfast and afternoon wine and snacks.

Château Versailles $$$ 65 rooms

1659 Rue Sherbrooke Ouest. 514-933-3611 or 888-933-8111. www.versailleshotels.com.

Fashioned from a row of elegant Golden Square Mile town houses, the Château Versailles is much the English manor hotel in Montreal. Salons and some rooms have wainscoting, elaborate fireplaces, moldings and chandeliers. Ground-floor rooms are decorated in cheerful colours but lack the period touches. The château lies at the start of a residential area, less noisy than elsewhere downtown, and only a few blocks from the Museum of Fine Arts and Rue Sainte-Catherine.

Holiday Inn Select $$$ 235 rooms

99 Ave. Viger Ouest. 514-878-9888 or 888-878-9888. www.yul-downtown.hiselect.com.

The house doctor is an acupuncturist, the gift shop sells lacquerware and vases, and the hotel's **Chez Chine ($$)** restaurant includes a pagoda and a huge water garden filled with colourful fish—along with excellent food. Altogether, you might forget that you're in Montreal. In fact, you're right in Chinatown, just steps from Old Montreal and Place des Arts.

Hôtel de la Montagne $$$ 135 rooms

1430 Rue de la Montagne. 514-288-5656 or 800-361-6262. www.hoteldelamontagne.com.

Hôtel de la Montagne is right in the midst of the restaurant and bar scene—it connects to **Les Beaux Jeudis (Thursday's) Restaurant ($$)** on Rue Crescent—and is consciously trendy, starting with the doorman in top hat. The hotel's more than show, however, with comfortable traditional furnishings in English or French country themes, and amenities that include a rooftop pool.

Hôtel de l'Institut $$$ 42 rooms

3535 Rue St-Denis. 514-282-5120 or 800-361-5111. www.ithq.qc.ca.

L'Institut is the hotel trade's counterpart to a teaching hospital. You'll get eager service from staffers who are learning the business, overseen by pros with years of experience. Although from the outside the building may look like a hospital, everything inside is freshly decorated, and the location along lively Rue Saint-Denis near the Latin Quarter couldn't be more tonic.

Must Stay: Montreal Hotels

Hôtel XIXe Siècle

$$$ 59 rooms

262 Rue St-Jacques Ouest. 514-985-0019 or 877-553-0019. www.hotelxixsiecle.com.

The "Nineteenth Century" Hotel combines attributes of Old Montreal's newer boutique hotels—a stately older bank building, ample grand spaces, softened formality and period charm—with more reasonable rates than elsewhere on this street. There usually isn't even a doorman on duty. Decorative updates in public areas are black-and-white, in subdued Art Deco style, while rooms are done in mid-19C French décor, accented with rattan pieces.

Hôtel Omni Mont-Royal

$$$ 300 rooms

1050 Rue Sherbrooke Ouest. 514-284-1110 or 888-444-6664. www.omnihotels.com.

A solid and respected doyenne, the Omni has maintained its quality and standards through several changes of identity (formerly Westin, formerly Four Seasons). You won't find idiosyncrasies or nooks and crannies, but rather, solid and reliable service, stately public areas with clean lines panelled in light marble, and amenities that include in-room Internet access and CD players. A rare treat is the heated outdoor pool, which is open all year. The location is convenient to McGill University and the central shopping area.

Hilton Montréal Aéroport

$$$ 486 rooms

12505 Côte-de-Liesse, Dorval. 514-631-2411 or 800-567-2411. www1.hilton.com.

Just minutes from the new terminal by free shuttle, the huge airport Hilton is surprisingly cheery on the inside, with sleekly styled renovated rooms, good restaurants, solarium health club, and a fair bit of local airline memorabilia. Landscaped grounds, an outdoor pool, and long-term parking add to the appeal. Express buses and commuter trains provide one-stop access to downtown.

Sofitel Montréal

$$$ 258 rooms

1155 Rue Sherbrooke Ouest. 514-285-9000 or 877-285-9001. www.sofitel.com.

From bright Provençal colours to serene marble bathrooms to the lobby with its wall-of-light reception desk, there is nothing that is not visually pleasing and soothing for the well-heeled business traveller at the Sofitel. No-pretense Art Moderne styling and excellent service will also attract those seeking a hotel experience not usually found on this continent. Amenities include a fitness centre and sauna, and high-speed Internet access, but no pool.

SpringHill Suites $$$ 124 rooms

445 Rue St-Jean-Baptiste. 514-875-4333 or 866-875-4333. www.springhillsuites.com.

The low-rise building of the Marriott SpringHill Suites hardly intrudes on Old Montreal. Inside, it's all modern and low-key, with predictable comforts including an indoor pool and garage, and a microwave and a refrigerator in the rooms. The new connects with the old: a passage leads to **Auberge St-Gabriel ($$$)**, one of the old city's more venerable restaurants, offering French and Quebec fare, such as *tourtiére* (meat pie) in informal surroundings in an old stone building.

Inexpensive

Angelica Blue Bed and Breakfast $$ 10 rooms

1213 Rue Ste-Elisabeth. 514-844-5048 or 800-878-5048. www.angelicablue.com.

The residential block of brick houses and wooden porches off busy Boulevard René-Lévesque is a surprise, and so is this guesthouse, with its friendly management and sunny, high-ceilinged rooms outfitted with down comforters, robes and hair dryers. You'll have to walk a couple of  blocks to anywhere, but "anywhere" includes Rue Saint-Denis and Place des Arts, the heart of Montreal's festival neighbourhood. Breakfast is included.

Anne ma soeur Anne Hôtel-Studio $$ 17 rooms

4119 Rue St-Denis. 514-281-3187 or 877-281-3187.
www.annemasoeuranne.com.

"Anne-my-sister-Anne" has more going for it than a mouthful of a name and virtual exclusivity as a lodging place in the trendy Plateau Mont-Royal area. Contemporary-style rooms have all been re-done, many with Murphy beds, and all with microwave and refrigerator, and high-speed Internet connection. The rate includes breakfast. There are some stairs to climb.

Auberge Bonsecours $$ 7 rooms

353 Rue St-Paul Est. 514-396-2662. www.aubergebonsecours.com.

Auberge Bonsecours carves cheery rooms in warm Provence yellows and reds, out of a small old warehouse set at the back of a renovated historic stable yard. Exposed brick and stone, sloping attic ceilings, and unexpected twists and corners add to the idiosyncratic charm of this inn, all nicely finished and maintained (and well air-conditioned in summer). Room rates for singles are quite a bit lower than the price for doubles, but either way, the price includes a buffet breakfast.

Auberge Le Jardin d'Antoine $$ 25 rooms

2024 Rue St-Denis. 514-843-4506 or 800-361-4506. www.hotel-jardin-antoine.qc.ca.

This nicely renovated town house expresses the gentility of bygone days, with polished woodwork and floral wallpaper and bedspreads. It's tranquil inside, despite the active street scene, and the rate includes a continental breakfast.

Hôtel St-Denis $$ 50 rooms

1254 Rue St-Denis. 514-849-4526 or 800-363-3364. www.hotel-st-denis.com.

Now into its ninth decade, the St-Denis has been renovated with care, while not putting on airs. Comfortable and well-lit, rooms are decorated with pieces that might have come from the local furniture store. And it's a safe haven in the Latin Quarter, where not all accommodations rent by the night.

Manoir Ambrose $$ 22 rooms

3422 Rue Stanley. 514-288-6922 or 888-688-6922. www.manoirambrose.com.

Can't afford to stay in the ritziest area of town? Think again. It's not the Ritz, but Manoir Ambrose, a series of connected town houses that provides odd-shaped rooms with old-style furnishings and personalized service is just steps from the Museum of Fine Arts. Continental breakfast is included in the rate.

Hôtel Castel Saint-Denis $ 18 rooms

2099 rue St-Denis, 514-842-9719. www.castelsaintdenis.qc.ca.

Here's an unpretentious hotel with just a few touches of style, such as wainscoted walls. It's clean and centrally air-conditioned, and rates as a "must" in the low-budget category.

Hotel Quartier Latin Montréal $ 40 rooms

1763 Rue St-Denis, 514-842-8444 or 866-843-8444. www.hotel-quartierlatin.com..

For bare-bones budget basic, you'll get more than you pay for at this hotel. Renovated modern rooms have private baths, and a continental breakfast each morning and the lively Latin Quarter location are included in the price.

Quebec City

Luxury

Auberge Saint-Antoine $$$$ 95 rooms

8 Rue St-Antoine. 418-692-2211 or 888-692-2211. www.saint-antoine.com.

The Saint-Antoine wraps 21C luxury inside an 18C warehouse in Lower Town. Rooms in both the original structure and the adjoining modern building boast exposed brick walls, comfortable modern styling, and down duvets and pillows. Large windows that open, free high-speed Internet access, and heated bathroom floors add thoughtful touches. Throughout the inn, the city's history lives on in the form of 18C artifacts displayed in glassed-in wall cases. Be sure to make reservations for a meal at **Panache** restaurant (**$$$**). Specializing in contemporary Canadian cuisine, Panache fills the charming space in the former warehouse's storage area.

Fairmont Le Château Frontenac $$$$ 618 rooms

1 Rue des Carrières. 418-692-3861 or 800-441-1414. www.fairmont.com/frontenac.

How does a hotel live up to its reputation as a landmark and national treasure? With self-assurance and every resort amenity, from spa to pool to tennis court, all set in pavilions built over generations—just like in a real castle. Elegant, panelled salons have welcomed prime ministers and royalty, and the staff is trained to extend equal deference to all guests, whether they stay in one of the standard value-priced rooms or in an executive suite. Casual **Café de la Terrasse ($$$)**, with its river views, offers breakfast, lunch, and dinner with a buffet as well as an à la carte menu option.

Moderate

Auberge St-Pierre $$$ 41 rooms

79 Rue St-Pierre. 418-694-7981 or 888-268-1017. www.auberge.qc.ca.

Sedate and sophisiticated, the St-Pierre incorporates new rooms built in individual style into the structure that once housed Canada's first insurance company. The contrasting Art Moderne fittings of other hotels in heritage quarters are shunned here. Most rooms have exposed brick walls, hardwood floors, print curtains, thick comforters and reproduction furniture that together suggest old Quebec. Bathrooms are modern, and Internet hook-up is provided.

Hôtel Le Priori $$$ 26 rooms

15 Rue Sault-au-Matelot. 418-692-3992 or 800-351-3992. www.hotellepriori.com.

On the trendier side of Lower Town, Le Priori fills a heritage stone building with a dignified stuccoed façade. It's located on a quiet street, a few blocks back from the river. Rooms vary in size as well as fittings; some come with claw-foot tubs out in the open, others with modern showers. **Restaurant Toast! ($$$)**, wraps around the lobby and opens into a private garden in warm weather; the cuisine is French.

Inexpensive

Hôtel Belley
$$ 15 rooms

249 Rue St-Paul. 418-692-1694 or 888-692-1694. www.oricom.ca/belley.

With its rustic brick façade and steep roof pierced with gables, the Belley looks every bit the tavern and lodging house that it has been for over a century and a half. It's been spruced up with modern lighting and works of art, but the tin ceilings and floors of octagonal tile exude the Olden Days. In the rooms, metal and black-and-white wood tables, chairs and beds play against exposed bricks and odd-shaped windows. The **bistro ($)** serves continental breakfast, micro brews and sandwiches.

Hôtel Le Saint-Paul
$$ 27 rooms

229 Rue St-Paul. 418-694-4414 or 888-794-4414. www.lesaintpaul.qc.ca.

This brick Queen Anne structure, with all its original nooks, crannies, low windows, and exposed brick walls, is located in the Old Port area of Lower Town, surrounded by antique shops. Features vary in the modestly priced rooms, but all have a full modern bath. **Peché Véniel Restaurant ($$)** is a light-filled Victorian salon that specializes in French cuisine.

Hôtel du Vieux Québec
$$ 41 rooms

1190 Rue St-Jean. 418-692-1850 or 800-361-7787. www.hvq.com.

Accommodation in Upper Town is pricey, but this wonderful exception features the charm of a 19C edifice and the feeling of being part of a vibrant Quebec City neighbourhood. Large rooms have adequate comforts, and some have cooking facilities. Rates go down the longer you stay, and rise to the $$$ range in summer.

Auberge Internationale de Québec
$ 62 rooms

19 Rue Ste-Ursule. 418-694-0755 or 800-461-8585. www.cisq.org.

Staying at Quebec City's youth hostel is not unlike a monastic experience. You're in a fine and substantial house in Upper Town, without frills or embellishment, but comfortable enough, with polished wood floors and simple furnishings. An on-site café and reading and games rooms encourage casual encounters. Private and family rooms are available.

Another Way to Look at It: Hotels by Theme

Looking for a place that will welcome you and your two toddlers? How about one that will pamper your darling chihuahua or dazzle you with stylish décor and magnificent views? In the previous pages we've organized the properties by price category; here we've arranged them by theme to help you find the perfect accommodations in Montreal and Quebec City.

Easy on the Budget
Angelica Blue Bed and Breakfast *(p 121)*
Anne ma soeur Anne Hôtel *(p 121)*
Hotel Castel Saint-Denis *(p 122)*
Hotel Quartier Latin Montréal *(p 122)*
Manoir Ambrose *(p 122)*
Auberge Internationale de Québec *(p 124)*

For Business Travelers
Hôtel Le Germain *(p 114)*
Fairmont The Queen Elizabeth *(p 115)*
Hilton Montréal Bonaventure *(p 115)*
Hotel InterContinental Montréal *(p 116)*
Hôtel Place d'Armes *(p 117)*
Hyatt Regency Montréal *(p 117)*
Hôtel Omni Mont-Royal *(p 120)*
Sofitel Montréal *(p 120)*
Fairmont Le Château Frontenac *(p 123)*

For Families
Fairmont The Queen Elizabeth *(p 115)*
Hyatt Regency Montréal *(p 117)*
Auberge de la Fontaine *(p 118)*
Holiday Inn Select *(p 119)*
SpringHill Suites *(p 121)*

Hotels with Hip Décor
Hôtel Gault *(p 116)*
Hotel St. Paul *(p 117)*
Hotel W Montréal *(p 117)*

Latin Quarter Hotels
Auberge de la Fontaine *(p 118)*
Hôtel de l'Institut *(p 119)*
Auberge Le Jardin d'Antoine *(p 122)*
Hotel Quartier Latin Montréal *(p 122)*
Hôtel Castel Saint-Denis *(p 122)*
Hôtel St-Denis *(p 122)*

Near Museums and Shopping
Hotel Le Germain *(p 114)*
Loews Hotel Vogue *(p 117)*
The Ritz-Carlton Montreal *(p 118)*
Château Versailles *(p 119)*
Hôtel de la Montagne *(p 119)*
Hôtel Omni Mont-Royal *(p 120)*
Manoir Ambrose *(p 122)*

Old Montreal Charm
Hostellerie Pierre du Calvet *(p 115)*
Hôtel Le Saint-Sulpice *(p 116)*
Hôtel Nelligan *(p 116)*
Hôtel Place d'Armes *(p 117)*
Auberge Bonaparte *(p 118)*
Auberge les Passants du Sans Soucy *(p 118)*
Auberge du Vieux-Port *(p 119)*
Auberge Bonsecours *(p 121)*

Old Quebec Charm
Auberge Saint-Antoine *(p 122)*
Auberge St-Pierre *(p 123)*
Hôtel Le Priori *(p 123)*
Hôtel Belley *(p 124)*
Hôtel Le Saint-Paul *(p 124)*

Posh Places
Hotel Le Germain *(p 114)*
Hotel Le St-James *(p 114)*
Hôtel Gault *(p 116)*
Hôtel Le Saint-Sulpice *(p 116)*
Hotel W Montréal *(p 117)*
Hôtel Place d'Armes *(p 117)*
The Ritz-Carlton Montreal *(p 118)*

State-of-the-Art Amenities
Hôtel Gault *(p 116)*
Hotel St. Paul *(p 117)*
Hotel W Montréal *(p 117)*
Hôtel Place d'Armes *(p 117)*
Loews Hotel Vogue *(p 117)*

Index

Index

Photo Credits:

Angelica Blue Bed and Breakfast
121; Anne ma soeur Anne Hôtel-
Studio 121; Association touristique
Laurentides, 96, 97; Auberge
Internationale de Quebec 124;
Auberge St-Pierre 123; Café du Monde
111; ©Canadian Tourism Commission,
Pierre St-Jacques 3, 7, 9, 18-19, 28, 37
62; © Casino de Montréal 66, 82; Chez
Queux 103, 113; Complexe Desjardins
29; ©Cosmodôme 73; Dawson College
63; Fairmont Le Château Frontenac
89, 123; Fairmont Queen Elizabeth
114-115; Ferreira Café 104; ©Festival
International de Jazz de Montréal,
Jean-François Leblanc 69; Hélène de
Champlain 106; Historic Urban Plans
20; Hotel Nelligan 116; Hotel XIX
Siècle 120; Insectarium de Montreal:
Michel Tremblay 70, André Payette
70; La Citadel de Quebec 91; Le
Méridien Versailles-Montréal 119, 125;
Le Petit Moulinsart 106, 113; Le Saint-
Amour 110; Le Taj 107; Les Remparts
102-103, 105; ©McCord Museum 43.

MICHELIN: 98, 100, 101; Gwen Cannon
88; Anne Culberson 49; Pierre Ethier
6, 7, 22, 26, 27, 28, 37, 48, 49, 50, 57, 60,
110; Doug Rogers 5, 86, 87, 88, 90, 92,
112, 124; Lili Thériault 24.

Notre Dame de Bonsecours Chapel,
Normand Rajotte 58; ©Parc Jean-
Drapeau: 4, 8, 71/Bob Burch 8,
Sébastian Larose 72, André Pichette
54, Eric St-Pierre 68; ©Parks Canada,
N. Rajotte 61; PhotoDisc© 84, 106,
108, 109, 113; Restaurant Le Vieux-Port
107; Ritz Carlton Hotel 5, 31, 118, 125;
Sofitel Montreal 120; Spa Eastman
85; Stewart Museum at the Fort 59;
St-Jeanne-de-Chantal 99; Théâtre
du Nouveau Monde 76; Toqué 103;
Tourisme Cantons-de-l'Est: 95, Pat &
Eden 93; Sylvain Majeau 94; Voodoo
Grill 112.

©Tourisme-Montréal: 34, 55; ©Auberge
de la Fontaine 118; ©Canadian Centre
for Architecture, Richard Bryant
47; ©Côpilia 42; Daniel Choinière
68; G. Duclos 9; Ecomusée du Fier
Monde 50; Pierre Girard 38; ©Inter-
Continental Montreal 116; ©Le
Bateau-Mouche au Vieux-Port, Yves
Binette 30; ©Les Descentes sur le
St-Laurent/Tourisme Montréal 7,
65; ©Les FrancoFolies, Jean-François
Leblanc 9, 77; ©Montreal Botanical
Garden 52; ©Montreal Museum
of Fine Arts, Prian Merrett 45;
Montréal Planetarium 51; ©Orchestre
Métropolitan 74; ©Omni 120; Stéphan
Poulin 4, 5, 6, 8, 21, 23, 25, 30, 31, 35, 39,
40, 44, 46, 56, 53, 64, 67, 78, 79, 80, 81;
©Hotel St-Paul 117, 125; Linda Turgeon
36, 104.

Cover photos:
Front Cover: © Tourisme Montréal,
Stéphan Poulin; Front Cover small
left: © The Montréal Dragon Boat
Race Festival; Front Cover small right:
© Parc Jean-Drapeau, Bernard Brault;
Back Cover: ©Tourisme Montréal,
Stéphan Poulin.